Gaslighting Recovery
for Women

Gaslighting Recovery

FOR WOMEN

The Complete Guide
to Recognizing Manipulation
and Achieving Freedom
from Emotional Abuse

Amelia Kelley, PhD

ZEITGEIST · NEW YORK

To the women in my life who have questioned their worth: Your voice matters, you matter, and you deserve to be loved and respected—simply because you are you.

Illustrations by Christy Ni
Chakra illustration (page 164) by Natalie Foss
Cover design by Aimee Fleck
Interior design by Katy Brown
Author photograph © by Jeannene Matthews, JR Photography
Edited by Kim Suarez

Printed in the United States of America
1st Printing

Contents

Introduction

Gaslighting is one of the most common forms of emotional abuse women can experience, worsening unbalanced power dynamics and societal and structural gender inequities. This form of emotional trauma can manifest in major areas of a woman's life, including romantic relationships, family, friendships, medical care, academia, professional roles, and within society at large.

As an integrative mental health therapist with a long-standing private practice, I have had the honor of working with a variety of women recovering from trauma. Though their stories and experiences differ, they all yearn for something similar—to be safe, seen, and heard. The mission statement for my practice is *"anyone who wants therapy receives therapy."* Making therapy or self-care tools accessible is my passion. With the right resources and tools, a great deal of healing can be done both in and outside of the therapy office. A crucial part of recovery from gaslighting is knowing you are not alone.

By learning to detect gaslighting, protect themselves, and become focused on self-care, women can overcome even the worst cases of gaslighting. When recovery work and healing remove the distortion that gaslighting creates, women discover that they are highly intuitive and emotionally strong. Their ability to persevere through a variety of challenges makes them a force to be reckoned with—a major deterring factor for those who want to control them.

Women who overcome gaslighting are able to regain control, heal, and thrive. Resilience is a common trait in those who have overcome gaslighting. Surviving this form of abuse creates an intuition and inner alarm system for all signs of gaslighting. Learning not to doubt themselves when they sense something is wrong, survivors establish a greater sense of self-worth and self-empowerment and no longer need to seek validation from others.

How to Use This Book

When reading this book, you are in control of your journey. Each chapter offers a range of therapy techniques, exercises, and tools, including journaling, skill-building worksheets, and self-care activities. If a portion of the book does not feel as relevant to you, you will likely still benefit from other chapters and can choose accordingly. If you are in the immediate throes of abuse or at the beginning of acknowledging your experience, I recommend that you start with Part One, Chapter 1. Also, taking breaks when needed is okay. Knowing and respecting your limits is a beautiful act of self-love.

This book is organized into three parts, beginning with identifying various forms of gaslighting and observing cases of women who have endured gaslighting themselves. From that foundation, you will be guided through exercises to help begin your healing and self-empowerment journey. Each part is key to recovering from gaslighting trauma.

Part One helps women understand and identify the different types of gaslighting that commonly occur in various relationships and dynamics, while also providing an action plan to establish safety. This chapter also explores different gaslighting cases, offering an opportunity to observe and learn from different women's experiences.

Part Two provides therapy exercises and techniques that facilitate personal healing through self-awareness of past traumas and unhealthy patterns—all with a focus on self-compassion and self-forgiveness. Before engaging in the activities, make sure you are not in a state of stress, such as feeling tired, hungry, or overwhelmed.

Part Three provides exercises and techniques rooted in generating self-esteem and self-love. You will learn to embrace who you truly are, while establishing an unbreakable sense of self-worth to help you navigate life with confidence and trust so that you can thrive in future relationships.

PART ONE
UNDERSTANDING GASLIGHTING

One of the greatest regrets in life is
being what others would want you
to be, rather than being yourself.

—SHANNON L. ALDER

Gaslighting breaks down a person's trust in oneself, causing self-doubt and confusion about personal opinions, self-awareness, and reality. Moreover, gaslighting can occur in any relationship (romantic, family, friends, coworkers) or within a group or organization (work, school, government, medical) where one has potential power over another or a group of others.

Gaslighting is not always obvious and often occurs in ways that are covert and difficult to detect. Understanding gaslighting effects and dynamics helps you connect with your true sense of self-worth, making it less likely someone will use gaslighting as a form of manipulation or emotional abuse against you. Gaslighting is most effective when it goes undetected, so having awareness is key in both prevention and recovery.

CHAPTER 1
What Is Gaslighting?

To fully understand what gaslighting is and the many forms it can take, this chapter provides crucial knowledge on the stages of gaslighting, the common motives for gaslighting, and the techniques and tactics used by a gaslighter. This chapter will also explore the reasons why women are more readily targeted than men. Because gaslighting is not as effective when identified and labeled, this chapter demonstrates how awareness is a powerful weapon to counteract it.

Origin

The term *gaslighting*, defined as manipulating someone by psychological means into questioning their own sanity, came from the 1938 British play *Gas Light*, which was later adapted into the 1944 MGM film *Gaslight*, starring Ingrid Bergman. The movie depicted a seemingly charming husband who slowly manipulates his wife through isolation and tactful deception in an attempt to make her lose her mind. In one example, he secretly knocked on the walls and dimmed the gas lighting in the house, all while insisting she was imagining things and declaring she was going insane. His actions were motivated by greed in an attempt to steal the family's jewels.

The term started entering therapists' offices in the mid-2010s as a descriptor for psychological manipulation in interpersonal relationships. The #MeToo movement in 2017 highlighted gaslighting of sexual abuse survivors, but still the term did not hit mainstream social media until 2018. Sociologists suggest that, in 2018, the term was popularized as a response to gaslighting occurring in politics, when some of the world's leaders lied to the public and outright denied things they had said or done. At the same time, there was a growing awareness of the importance of normalizing mental health and equity in relationships.

The Gaslighter

The need for power is the most common motive for gaslighting. Being raised by a gaslighter can cause a loss of autonomy and power as early as childhood, and the victims of gaslighting may likely adopt the same gaslighting techniques as a means of survival. For those individuals who did not experience gaslighting in their past, the need for power can stem from insecurities and self-esteem issues present in narcissists or other antisocial individuals. While narcissism has a clear correlation to gaslighting, not everyone who gaslights is a narcissist.

Non-narcissistic gaslighting can present itself in people trying to advance professionally or socially (politicians, medical professionals, cult leaders, government figures, or those trying to sustain gender and/or race disparity) without consideration for the well-being of their victim.

Narcissistic gaslighting is wrought with emotional invalidation and degradation of a sense of self. According to Shahida Arabi, author, academic, and long-standing researcher on the topic of narcissim, "Narcissists are masters of making you doubt yourself and the abuse." Narcissistic gaslighting is motivated by a planned effort to gain control and power over another by increasing self-doubt and dependence on the gaslighter. When done successfully, the gaslighter, having altered the victim's sense of reality, becomes a false source of security, thus increasing the trauma bond.

DID YOU KNOW?

The term *gaslighting* was Merriam-Webster's 2022 word of the year. The term had a 1740 percent spike in searches that year, with no precipitating event—meaning there was no "trending event" that drove the searches, rather just an organic growth in interest. This was not the first time *gaslighting* was up for word of the year. In 2018, it was among the runners-up but was beat out by the word *toxic*, which encompassed a broader scope of negative behaviors. While gaslighting is a toxic behavior, it is possible for someone to be toxic and not be gaslighting. Common behaviors of a toxic person that can be exclusive from gaslighting include being unsupportive, judgmental, self-centered, and controlling.

The key difference between toxicity and gaslighting is that gaslighting is used as a means to disturb and change how the other person feels about their sense of reality, while toxicity can exist in other forms of unhealthy or abusive behaviors.

WOMEN AND GASLIGHTING

Women can be extremely powerful and intuitive—a realization that can be intimidating to people or groups who want to control them. Women, generally speaking, are emotionally aware and sensitive to the needs of others, while also being pragmatic and decisive. While emotional awareness and sensitivity are incredible assets to society, certain patriarchal systems have tried to diminish these skills by labeling women as "too sensitive" or "overly emotional."

Patriarchy thrives off gaslighting women as a means to sustain power over them. In Melinda Wenner Moyer's *New York Times* article "Women Are Calling Out Medical Gaslighting," she outlines the issue of medical gaslighting that has existed long before there was a term to describe it. For centuries, women have been told they were suffering "hysteria" in response to almost all mental health issues as well as any medical issues related to the uterus. Women's health and bodily autonomy have been sidelined, while research, financial investment, and future treatment options historically prioritized men's health. As a result, men's health issues are more readily focused on, benefitting them over women—though excluding women from medical research eventually becomes harmful to both genders.

Gaslighting Techniques and Tactics

A variety of gaslighting tactics can be used by abusers. The following are seven of the most harmful and common gaslighting techniques to look out for. Some gaslighters will employ them all, while others will focus on specific tactics. It is important to note that the presence of just one tactic, whether once or over a period of time, can signal an issue.

A GAP IN THE RESEARCH

While particular people, groups, and systems benefit from gaslighting women, there are negative repercussions that harm our society as a whole. Medical gaslighting has created a gap in the research necessary for treating serious illnesses. Heart disease, for example, presents differently in women than in men, but diagnostic tools for this disease are based on research primarily focused on men, which results in medical professionals often overlooking life-threatening symptoms present in women. Our mothers, daughters, sisters, and friends deserve the same medical care, respect, and attention as the rest of society, because when they suffer, we all suffer.

1. **Denial** is when a person refuses to take responsibility for their actions, even at times when there is evidence they are at fault. Pretending to forget details, blame-shifting, or outright lying are all examples of denial.

2. **Withholding** involves *strategic incompetence*, where the person pretends they do not understand or hear what someone is saying. The gaslighter will claim they never heard the other person or diminish them by saying they do not make any sense. This is done in a way that suggests the other person is illogical or confusing. Another example may be the gaslighter accusing their victim of being a poor listener if they do not remember something the gaslighter said.

3. **Trivializing** occurs when someone is made to feel that what they think or want is just "too much." Being called overemotional, dramatic, or demanding when someone is expressing themselves are signs of trivializing. As previously mentioned in medical gaslighting, women's

various medical needs historically being labeled as "hysteria" is an example of this form of gaslighting.

4. **Diverting** is when someone questions the credibility of another person by questioning their source of information—for instance, telling someone "you don't know what you're talking about because you get all your information off the internet." Unfortunately, the circulation of misinformation and institutional gaslighting (otherwise known as systemic abuse by large entities such as educational institutions, churches, corporations, or the government) make this technique even more effective.

5. **Countering** questions someone's memory of events as a way to instill doubt, even when there is evidence to confirm that memory. The gaslighter will question whether the other person is forgetting what really happened and often creates a narrative that the victim has a bad memory or "always forgets how things happened." This gaslighting tactic was evident in the film *Gaslight*, when the husband outright denied or questioned his wife's memory of what was happening.

6. **Stereotyping** weaponizes negative stereotypes concerning gender, race, ethnicity, sexuality, nationality, or age. With stereotyping, overgeneralizing becomes a tool to predict or explain why the targeted person may be wrong, crazy, too angry, too emotional, or hard to believe.

7. **Deflecting** happens when the gaslighter is confronted with evidence of wrongdoing, and rather than acknowledging what they did, the gaslighter regains control by bringing up something the other person has done wrong. When the gaslighter feels attacked by being confronted with tangible proof (a recording of a conversation, receipt, or e-mail), they will counterattack by demoralizing the other person for being untrusting, jealous, insensitive, evil, heartless, and so forth for bringing the issue up in the first place.

7 COMMON GASLIGHTING TECHNIQUE PHRASES

Denial	*"I never did that / said that / thought that / wanted that."*
Withholding	*"You need to speak up."* *"You make no sense."* *"You talk too fast."*
Trivializing	*"Why are you so needy / emotional / hysterical / ridiculous / overdramatic / negative?"*
Diverting	*"You can't believe everything you read / hear / see."* *"I would never believe what ___ says (insert any organization, political group, or belief system the gaslighter does not align with)."*
Countering	*"You totally do not remember what happened. You have such a bad memory. This is what happened . . ."* *"I can never trust your memory."* *"You just make things up because you can't remember what really happened."*
Stereotyping	*"They won't believe you because they never believe women when they report abuse."* *"You don't really know what you are talking about because you are too young to understand."*
Deflecting	*"Why are you bringing this up when you are the one who is to blame for our issues?"* *"How can you complain about this when you don't even care about me? You never have."* *"You are just being petty."*

The Stages of Gaslighting

In *Psychology Today*, Preston Ni outlines and summarizes the seven stages of gaslighting as identified in a variety of research studies on the topic. Not all instances of gaslighting will progress in the same order or cover all the same stages. Just as relationships vary, so too do progressions of gaslighting.

STAGE 1: LIES AND EXAGGERATION

Gaslighting starts with the gaslighter creating a false negative narrative about their target. Nothing is off-limits at this stage as the gaslighter searches for what makes their target most insecure. For example, a wife arrives home late from work. The gaslighting husband exaggerates by saying, "You're always late; you obviously don't care about me at all." This causes the wife to defend herself as she is thrown into a negative feedback loop about not caring for her husband.

STAGE 2: REPETITION IS KEY

If stage 1 only happened once (perhaps when a partner was feeling tired, defensive, or insecure), the behavior is unlikely to progress into emotional abuse and gaslighting. But if the goal is to control the other person, the behavior has to be repeated. Women have often experienced repetitive gaslighting in our patriarchal systems, which is why they are more likely to get roped into this destructive cycle.

STAGE 3: ESCALATE WHEN CHALLENGED

When the gaslighter is confronted about their behavior, they will react by doubling down on their gaslighting techniques. Their denial will be so incredulous that the target will experience doubt and negative emotions. The gaslighter will deny responsibility and focus on how hurt they are to be accused of something they did not do (often despite hard evidence). The gaslighter will attempt to capitalize off the empathy of their target, and also try to lay blame upon the target for causing their hurt.

STAGE 4: WEAR DOWN THEIR TARGET

The most effective way for a gaslighter to sustain control over their target is to strip them of their identity and sense of reality. In this stage, the gaslighter will remain on the offense to wear down the emotional energy of their victim, increasing the victim's self-doubt so they will further align with the distorted reality created by the gaslighter.

STAGE 5: CODEPENDENCY

At this stage, the target begins to rely on the gaslighter for acceptance, approval, respect, and safety. The gaslighter will leverage this power by threatening to take desired dynamics away any time the gaslightee does not agree with them. If the gaslighter believes they are losing control of their victim, they will employ fear and vulnerability to keep their victim attached to them.

THE RELATIONSHIP SLOT MACHINE

Intermittent reward (giving false hope) is so powerful that it is employed as a coercive control tactic in the most extreme cases of trauma bonding. Research done at the John Jay College of Criminal Justice found it to be so effective that it was a key component in sex trafficking. Our neurobiology responds favorably to intermittent rewards, especially when they are unpredictable, with a burst of feel-good hormones such as dopamine and serotonin. The experience can be so rewarding that other negative aspects of a relationship become tuned out. Much like gambling, we wouldn't sink money into a slot machine if there were *no* chance of winning, but the *chance* of a payout is enough to keep us hooked. The same goes for toxic relationships.

STAGE 6: GIVING FALSE HOPE

Without hope, there is little investment, and the gaslighter knows this. To keep their victim hooked, the gaslighter will intermittently supply superficial kindness or remorse. As a result, the victim questions their gut instinct as to whether things are "really that bad," and these feelings of self-doubt further connect them to the gaslighter. Instilling false hope is part of the abuse cycle, reinforcing the idea that things may change for the better, even when this is not true.

STAGE 7: DOMINATE AND CONTROL

The final stage, and the ultimate goal of gaslighting, is to gain complete control over how an individual, or group, feels and behaves. By now, the gaslighter has completely altered the gaslightee's sense of reality and can weaponize their tactics at will. The gaslighter will exploit their victim in any way that serves their agenda to remain in control. This leaves their victim in a constant state of insecurity, doubt, and fear.

Gaslighting Effects

Gaslighting can have a lasting impact on an individual's self-esteem and mental health, as well as their trust in others and themselves. The negative impact of gaslighting can vary for each individual and their unique situation. The following are some of the more common long-term effects.

TRUST ISSUES

Gaslighting seeks to destroy someone's trust in themselves and, at times, can also destroy the ability to feel safe with other people, groups, or entities. As if experiencing gaslighting in the present moment was not enough, the mistrust cycle ends up hurting the survivor further in the future. A survivor of gaslighting may be less likely to seek support for medical, educational, professional, or interpersonal issues, if they struggle to believe anyone will help them.

MENTAL HEALTH ISSUES

The goal of gaslighting is to make the target feel mentally disordered, and sometimes it works. A loss of control and confidence, isolation, and chronic stress from gaslighting all have a negative impact on the way we think. Unhealthy thinking patterns increase self-doubt, self-loathing, and insecurities—qualities which are all commonly found in depression, anxiety, and other mood disorders. Thoughts are powerful, and when someone experiences chronic negative thoughts—falling into a self-negating pattern—they are more likely to struggle with these mental health issues.

TRAUMA RESPONSE

Research conducted at Cambridge University on long-term cultural gaslighting found that, the longer a person or group experienced gaslighting, the more prevalent generational trauma and societal inequities become. Post-traumatic stress disorder (PTSD) occurs when there is an unhealthy response to a traumatic situation. Emotional abuse from gaslighting poses a greater risk for someone to not only develop PTSD but, more specifically, complex PTSD (cPTSD), a form of PTSD resulting from repeated or prolonged interpersonal trauma.

What differentiates cPTSD are *disturbances in self-organization (DSO)* in the following areas:

- **Emotional regulation**, which is the ability to effectively manage and respond to emotional experiences. When regulated, an individual can remain socially connected and have a perceived tolerance for emotions as they arise.

- **Negative self-concept**, which makes it difficult to identify and seek out personal wants and needs. Accepting criticism, advice, or ideas that are contrasting to one's own can be difficult as well. There may also be a sense of disconnection from the self, which negatively impacts confidence in the ability to meet challenges.

- **Interpersonal difficulties**, which develop in a variety of ways but often make it difficult to connect authentically with others, making trust and intimacy difficult.

Understanding the nuances of cPTSD offers women who have experienced gaslighting answers about why they may be struggling and the language to ask for what they need from those who support them (for example, in therapy, they may benefit from dialectical behavior therapy, or DBT, to improve emotional regulation).

IDENTIFYING COMPLEX PTSD (CPTSD)

The following are symptoms that can be present in both PTSD and cPTSD:

- **Re-experiencing:** where the victim relives the event in the form of flashbacks and obsessive thoughts of the trauma.

- **Avoidance/Numbing:** where the person may avoid people, places, or situations reminiscent of their trauma, often causing detachment from others.

- **Hyperarousal:** a state of being constantly alert, having a heightened startle response, feeling on edge, experiencing panic attacks and/or chronic pain issues from tension.

CHAPTER 2

Family

This chapter focuses on cases of women gaslit by family members, and how family dynamics with the gaslighter affect them. The cases are gathered from the experiences of real clients who I have been honored to work with, learn from, and grow with. Each case highlights tactics used by the abuser as well as characteristics of these toxic relationships. Because family abuse can happen in a variety of relationships, each case will explore unique roles and relationship dynamics.

"The Overprotective Father"

Crystal was in her early 30s and first came to my office because of her issues with commitment, low self-esteem, and a pervasive hypochondria around an intense fear of contracting STDs or becoming pregnant, despite being a virgin. Crystal was the oldest of three children. Her youngest sibling died at birth, when Crystal was just four years old, leaving her with one brother.

At the time, her father refused to process the traumatic loss of his child; he avoided therapy and rarely spoke about what happened. Instead, he processed his pain by choosing to "overprotect" his only living daughter, while ignoring much of the early child experiences for his son. Some of Crystal's earliest memories are of her father telling her that, without his protection, she was at risk of being hurt or taken advantage of. He wanted control over all her decisions. Crystal could not choose her friends, her clothes, her hobbies, or even what she wanted to do for school projects without first getting her father's opinion. If Crystal expressed her own thoughts, he would tell her that she had "no idea what she was talking about" and would *stereotype* her by saying "she was too young to understand what she really wanted so she needed his help."

As her therapist, I observed that Crystal was highly intelligent and thoughtful in conversations, but she doubted her intelligence and struggled to trust herself with making decisions. His repeated efforts to break down her confidence altered her sense of self and beliefs; she considered herself to be inept and unable to care for herself, further increasing her codependency with him.

When Crystal developed interest in dating during her teen years, he weaponized their religious faith and lied by saying that even thinking about dating was a sin and that she would most certainly contract STDs or become pregnant if she was ever intimate with a boy—even kissing would put her at risk. He shamed her any time she wanted to wear clothing that showed her figure. To appease him, she would wear loose-fitting clothing to hide her body, but still he persisted in calling her a "tease" even if she was wearing a loose sweater and jeans. She constantly felt criticized. His persistent gaslighting led her to become terrified of getting pregnant and never feeling comfortable with dating or seeking out intimate connections with men. She was never able to confront her father about how he impacted her because, when she was in her mid-twenties, he was diagnosed with pancreatic cancer and died shortly after.

Finally, released from the physical bond to her father and having to justify and explain her choices, Crystal sought out therapy. Since then, she has been working on her obsessive-compulsive fears around physical intimacy. The persistent emotional manipulation impacted her ability to enjoy sex and she sought out pelvic floor physical therapy to retrain her body to let go of her negative self-concept and finally enjoy a healthy, consensual, sexual relationship. Despite the evidence that she was capable and had made a series of healthy choices in her life, Crystal still struggled with an intensely negative self-concept, making it difficult to determine her wants and needs, because for so long she was dependent on her father for all her life choices.

CASE 2
"The Neglected Mother"

Joy was an early-20-something-year-old girl who worked as an advocate for female abuse victims. She was engaged and shared a loving home with her fiancé and their dog, Leroy. Joy drew in those around her with her friendly and positive personality.

Despite all her positive traits, Joy suffered the long-term effects of gaslighting. Ever since childhood, Joy had worked to win the approval of her mother. Joy's mother was a beautiful and accomplished businesswoman who also suffered from unexplained health issues, and Joy felt blamed for them. "My mother would tell me that my not calling her enough or being sympathetic enough was the reason she was so sick.

She fixated on the stress I caused by not being close enough to her, even though talking to her at times made me sick to my stomach. I started to believe her flare-ups could be my fault because I too felt ill any time I thought about her."

Every time Joy visited her family, she felt on edge. One particular visit led to a serious case of vertigo that caused her to miss work. During that visit, her mother *trivialized* every emotion Joy felt in front of the entire family, bringing up every mistake she ever made, calling Joy lazy for struggling in school (mainly due to undiagnosed ADHD that she would discover in her adulthood). Her mother said Joy was unable to help herself because Joy was "too needy," which was a catchphrase to describe Joy as early as the age of five. To avoid the appearance of being "too needy," Joy concealed her feelings and trauma from her mother and other family members. When she was sexually assaulted in high school, Joy did not report the assault or ask for the help she deserved. This led to a string of unhealthy relationships where she was emotionally abused and taken for granted.

Joy struggled with mental health issues and was diagnosed with ADHD, bipolar disorder, and generalized anxiety disorder. She had an intensely negative self-concept and often spoke of and to herself in a critical tone. She spent numerous sessions in tears about what a disappointment she was, despite support from people around her who continually reminded her that she was loved and wanted. Joy cornered herself into a rejection cycle, where she would continually fail at things she set out to do, perpetuating her negative self-concept.

When she moved away from home, Joy felt the fog of gaslighting lift just enough to get her college degree, find a meaningful career, and build a few special, loving relationships. Still, she suffered from low self-esteem, poor body image, and constantly compared herself to others. Her downward spirals in adulthood were provoked by phone calls and visits she had with her mother.

Presently Joy is learning that it is not her responsibility to pick up the phone whenever her mother calls and that boundaries are an essential part of her self-care. It is difficult for Joy to imagine not having a relationship with her mother, and Joy's inability to let go is one of the reasons the gaslighting has persisted for as long as it has.

CASE 3
"The Betrayed Daughter"

Sasha was a natural empath. She felt strongly for all people and animals around her and did everything she could to make sure they were alright. She fed stray cats in the neighborhood, sometimes being the only one who showed them any affection, and she was the first to offer help if a friend or family member was in need. Her sensitive nature was cultivated at an early age when her parents, immigrants from Eastern Europe, worked long hours and left Sasha and her four siblings home alone. Her older sister Anna was left in charge, and she did the bare minimum required to care for her siblings and was cold most of the time.

Anna had qualities Sasha envied—she was beautiful, popular, and well-liked—but Anna had a dark side unseen by most. She would physically abuse herself by cutting, binge drinking, and repeatedly threatening suicide. Though their parents were concerned about Anna, they were not present, and so agreeable and empathetic Sasha made an easy target for Anna to vent her pain to.

The sisters' relationship remained tumultuous until Sasha moved away from home. For years, Sasha never returned except to attend the funeral for her father and then her mother, 15 years later. Prior to her death, Anna would verbally and emotionally abuse her mother, yelling at her in their native language, calling her stupid, and blaming her for everything that went wrong in her life.

After their mother died, Anna's abuse was directed at Sasha. Sasha reported that her sister would create false narratives, especially when she was drinking, accusing Sasha of wanting Anna to kill herself. Her sister would call all hours of the day and leave voicemails saying it would be

Sasha's fault if Anna went through with it. Any attempt Sasha made to defend herself or confront her sister was met with further *denial* tactics from Anna, who claimed she never said any of those things.

As much as Sasha tried to reassure herself that the accusations were unfounded, the fear of Anna potentially following through with the suicidal threats was gripping. Anna was tactful and knew better than to push too hard, as she would use her charming personality to lure Sasha back in whenever she was sober. She would ask Sasha (who was too kind to say no) to help her purchase things off the internet, as she did not have a computer in her home, and would reward the gestures with intense affirmation and what appeared to be genuine love. This never lasted long before the relationship became toxic again. Anna craved the comfort of the trauma bond, and Sasha needed to be relieved of the incredible guilt her sister had convinced her to carry in her heart. The two sisters still waver between codependency, false hope, domination, and fleeting moments of radio silence.

SUMMARY AND CONCLUSION
When Family Members Gaslight

Gaslighting that occurs in family relationships is difficult to get away from and tends to persist for years, if not a lifetime. Family gaslighters can be anyone—primary caregivers or parents, siblings, extended family, or stepfamily. The one thing that is constant, however, is the complexity of the entire family system and how it plays a role in the gaslighting dynamic.

When an entire family bears witness to gaslighting and no one protects the victim, often out of fear of being targeted themselves, it can further perpetuate the distorted version of reality painted by the gaslighter. To help defend against family gaslighting, you will find a safety plan below that outlines necessary steps—including seeking support from others as well as professionals. Connecting with healthy individuals not influenced by the gaslighter can help you with regaining a sense of reality, identifying potential danger that has become tolerated over time, and provides you with a support structure if boundary setting with a gaslighter poses any threat. Having outside support helps victims to take positive steps toward setting healthy boundaries and moving forward in the healing journey after experiencing gaslighting abuse from a family member.

One thing I often tell clients who grapple with family gaslighting is this: Just because they are your family does not mean they have to remain in your life. It is okay to decide someone is too toxic for you to spend time with, even if they are family.

ESTABLISHING SAFETY

An action-oriented plan protects you from gaslighting, especially in complicated situations, such as a family relationship where the abuser is unavoidable or difficult to escape. Below is a step-by-step plan to follow if you believe you are being gaslit.

Step 1: Identify the Gaslighting. The first and most crucial step involves recognizing what is happening. Pay attention to any common phrases and tactics being used. Notice if the situation causes:

- Self-doubt, confusion, and/or uncertainty
- Over-apologizing
- Insecurity about the validity of your feelings
- Difficulty with decision-making
- Feeling a loss of control

Step 2: Create Space. If you live with a gaslighter, try spending less time at home. Get a job, sign up for after-school or after-work activities, leave home for exercise purposes like a walk or run, and spend time with other friends or family. If this is not possible, create space in your body with breathwork, grounding exercises, and other skills explored in Part Three of this book.

Step 3: Gather Evidence. Documentation can help ground your sense of reality and help with future decision-making about the relationship. Collect photos, texts, emails, and so forth. The documentation is *not* intended to change the gaslighter as they will likely weaponize the evidence. Instead, it is a connection to your true sense of reality and a grounding reminder of your thoughts and feelings separate from the gaslighter.

Step 4: Involve a Supportive Person. Sharing your experience with others may feel scary, but it can also save you from future harm. Find people to trust outside of the relationship to help you regain reality and, when appropriate, create a plan to either confront the gaslighting or remove yourself from it.

When gaslighting exists in an inescapable abusive relationship, it may be necessary to seek professional support. One option is calling the National Domestic Violence Hotline at 1-800-799-7233.

Intimate Relationships

On the topic of gaslighting, it's common to first think of romantic partnerships. This is due to the intimate nature of these relationships and the extensive time partners tend to spend together. Chapter 3 explores real cases of women gaslit by romantic partners, and how the abuse affected their self-esteem, self-worth, and, at times, overall safety. We will also touch on healthy boundary setting and the cycle of abuse, both crucial in understanding how to prevent potentially abusive relationships from escalating.

CASE I
"The Lonely Fiancé"

Sarah and Jill had been engaged for five years when Sarah began therapy to address motivation issues, intense anxiety, and insomnia. When asked about her relationship, Sarah said she was postponing wedding planning because something felt "off." Despite wanting to postpone, her fiancé, Jill, had been actively pressuring Sarah to move forward and said if Sarah hesitated, she had no reason to stay around.

I asked Sarah to describe how friends and family viewed her and Jill as a couple, but she said she didn't know because "Jill doesn't really like people." Before meeting Jill, Sarah was extremely social and had several close friends, coworkers, and family she enjoyed spending time with. Since meeting Jill, Sarah's social support system quickly dwindled. Anytime Sarah wanted to spend time with someone separately (such as seeing friends at her rock-climbing gym or going out for a drink after work with her team), Jill would accuse Sarah of caring about other people more than her. Sarah really loved Jill and wanted the relationship to work, so she tried everything she could to convince Jill of her loyalty to her. She started canceling plans with friends and even gave up her rock-climbing group.

As time went on, the accusations became more inflamed. Jill would accuse Sarah of cheating whenever Sarah was texting or emailing a friend or coworker. When Sarah tried to defend herself, Jill *deflected* by accusing Sarah of "trying to stress her out," leading Sarah to apologize for bringing up her concerns. Sarah reported feeling nervous when she received an email or text, and so she began sneaking around if she needed to respond to a conversation. The dishonesty made her question her fidelity and she began experiencing anxiety, difficulty sleeping, and migraines. The fewer people that were in her life, the more dependent Sarah became on Jill, and she found herself agreeing to almost anything her fiancé wanted.

When Sarah had been approached about an amazing job opportunity that would send her back into the office and almost double her salary and status in her field, Jill berated her for caring more about money than spending time with her and again threatened to leave. Sarah turned down the job. While Sarah wanted to be with her fiancé, she could not shake the feeling that, in doing so, she had lost herself.

BOUNDARY SETTING AND THE MYTH OF THE "PERFECT TIME"

Nedra Glover Tawwab, author of *Set Boundaries, Find Peace: A Guide to Reclaiming Yourself,* says that when you first become uncomfortable in a relationship or life circumstance, it is a good indicator a boundary is needed. "No" is a full sentence, and you do not need to justify a boundary—it is yours to own. However, too many people postpone boundary setting out of fear of hurting others. However, procrastination creates blurred boundaries and sends the message that others can take advantage of you. The myth of the "perfect time" existed in Sarah and Jill's relationship when Sarah was berated any time she shared concerns when Jill was "not in the mood." In reality, Sarah was never allowed to express herself, no matter the timing.

It is very common for a gaslighter to use the "timing" of your boundary as an excuse to attack. They may say something along the lines of "Why did you have to bring this up now?" or "You always come at me right when I get home from work!" or, quite simply, "Your timing sucks." It is not okay for the gaslighter to use the "perfect time" myth against you. Your boundaries matter *all* the time.

"The Narcissistic Abuser"

Mary is a nurse and mother to a baby boy. She first met Ryan when they were both in their early 20s—about 10 years ago. At the time, Ryan had an issue with drinking, and she decided he was not a healthy person for her. They broke up and Mary went on to marry someone else.

Mary's first marriage ended. During therapy, she reported feeling insecure about the passage of time and her desire to have children. Soon, Ryan resurfaced and the stage was set for his love bombing and extreme displays of affection to hook her back into a relationship. Ryan promised he was a changed man and loved Mary and wanted the family they were always meant to have. He knew exactly what to say, being aware of Mary's fear of never becoming a mother. Less than a year later, they were married.

Shortly after the wedding, Ryan's behavior shifted. He began drinking again, and started blaming Mary for his bad moods. Any time she stood up to him, he would remind her of the past, when she had broken up with him. He fixated on his fear of her abandoning him, creating the narrative that she was not as faithful as him. Just as his displays of jealousy were starting to intensify, Mary became pregnant with their first child.

There was a brief period of false hope after their son's birth. Ryan's drinking stopped for about two months, and they both focused solely on the baby. This did not last long; Ryan began to vie for Mary's attention any time she was focused on the baby. His drinking increased, as did his lies. When Mary confronted him about the drinking, he would employ *denial* tactics, even with blatant evidence of empty bottles in the garage. Ryan said she was causing him stress and, as a result, he stopped helping her around the house, and the home environment suffered. He would yell at her and blame her for being a slob and not caring about the well-being of their child.

Mary wanted to leave Ryan, but he threatened to kill himself if she ever left and said it would be her fault. The situation escalated. That night,

Mary decided to leave. While loading their child into the car, she heard a gunshot. She fell to her knees in fear that Ryan had followed through with his threat. She called the police to search her home, and they found Ryan very much alive. Later, Ryan was angry that she had "made something out of nothing and created such a chaotic situation." He *deflected* blame onto her for the police arriving and said if he lost his job, it would be her fault.

The cops admitted Ryan into a psychiatric hospital and, when she went to pick him up two days later, he accused her of being a bad mother, a bad Christian, and a bad wife, saying if she tried harder, the marriage would be salvageable. They went home, unsure of their future as a couple, but still very much together. He inflated her insecurities until she started to believe they were true.

CASE 3
"The Loyalist"

Melinda came to therapy because she felt disconnected from herself. She struggled with autoimmune issues and experienced chronic stress from her blended family dynamics. She and her husband, Peter, had children from their previous marriages and together they had created a new family. During the course of therapy, she received a medical diagnosis from her primary doctor that finally allowed her to receive treatment. Her health improved, but she still could not determine the cause of her stress. In therapy, Melinda and I discussed the concept of "walking on eggshells," where a victim works hard not to upset an emotional abuser, and she recognized that the core of her chronic stress was rooted in her constant attempts not to upset her husband.

Her insecurities began prior to her current marriage, as Melinda carried tremendous guilt from her first divorce. Because of this, she was steadfast in making her current marriage work. Peter was charming, well-spoken, and assertive; he always had a quick response in the face of a conflict. They argued regularly and it often centered around him accusing her of being disloyal. Peter fixated on the idea that her wanting to visit her adult children from her previous marriage without him was a betrayal. He *trivialized* her desire to see her children and accused her of choosing them over him, saying "he would never do that to her." If he was upset with one of their children, which happened often, he would tell her that a good wife would side with him no matter what. When she refused, he would stonewall her, or purposely ignore her, to inflict punishment.

Peter's behavior was confusing because he regularly employed promises of hope and moments of peace. He could even be quite helpful and romantic at times. He knew she was sensitive, and that the relationship would end if he was always being destructive. He would elaborate on how much he loved her and convince her that the only reason he acted the way he did was because she meant so much to him. He countered her feelings and *diverted* any time she expressed frustration, telling her "I would never question you"—even though he did regularly. He would then try to reconnect with her through physical intimacy, even if she did not seem interested. Above all else, he would never apologize.

Because the cycle of emotional abuse continues to be so masterfully orchestrated, Melinda still feels she cannot leave the marriage. Almost monthly, as if on schedule, she is manipulated by Peter's intermittent rewards of love and promises to change. These efforts refocus her on fixing *her* approach to their problems, which *he* in fact has created. His tactic is to keep her interested, hopeful, confused, and on the defense, and so far, he is succeeding.

SUMMARY AND CONCLUSION
The Cycle of Abuse

Hope that develops from the empty promises for change are the key to sustained gaslighting abuse in intimate relationships. Moments of relief from stress can work to create a false sense of control and a belief that the gaslighter can be changed, and without this hope the relationship would likely not continue. Deflecting and blame shifting, while used as aggressive gaslighting tactics, can also be used to create a false sense of control in the gaslightee. The person being gaslit may feel that they can somehow "fix" the situation if they just become everything their partner wants and needs. In the process of doing so, they lose themselves.

As a trauma-informed therapist who works with survivors of abuse, I am often asked, "How does one know if they are in an abusive relationship?" The most common sign to watch for is whether one feels a loss of control over their life and their identity. Each of the cases explored in this chapter involved someone giving up something they wanted. Sarah gave up a job opportunity, Mary gave up the hope of leaving and raising her son in peace, and Melinda gave up seeing her adult children. Before giving up even more of oneself, it is beneficial to understand the classic abuse cycle—and to then make an informed decision.

THE CYCLE OF ABUSE INCLUDES FOUR STAGES:

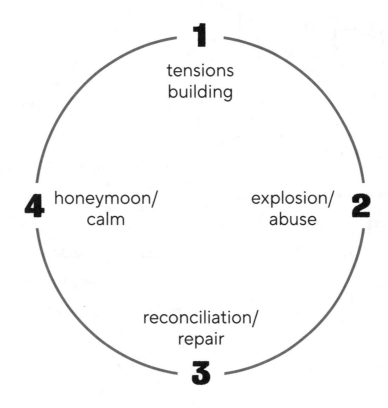

1 tensions building

2 explosion/abuse

3 reconciliation/repair

4 honeymoon/calm

CHAPTER 4
Society

While gaslighting often happens on a personal level between people, it can also occur in a public arena when a person or group is trying to marginalize another. Stereotypes that keep women disempowered lead to them being commonly targeted in instances of societal gaslighting. Societal gaslighting occurs in a variety of settings including work places, academia, government, media, medical institutions, and an array of other societal constructs. This chapter specifically dives into cases of women being gaslit in various areas of society, as well as the negative impact on these individual women.

CASE I
"Dr. Google and the Pregnant Mother"

Leah was nearing 35 when she became pregnant with her first child. She and her husband had been trying for years and they were thrilled and grateful to be pregnant again, while still cautiously optimistic due to prior miscarriage and loss.

Leah believed her thyroid disease had a negative impact on their fertility journey. She had researched the disease extensively after her last miscarriage and was confident that taking progesterone suppositories could help her current pregnancy thrive. It appeared the medication posed little harm while the benefit could be a healthy pregnancy.

At six weeks, she scheduled an appointment to confirm the pregnancy. She discussed her concern with her doctor, who said she would have to do a blood test and adamantly refused to prescribe anything until eight weeks. He then used the tactic of *diverting* her knowledge by saying that "she can't rely on the internet for medical knowledge" and that "he went to a much better college than Dr. Google." She didn't laugh at his joke and, when she sat quietly looking hurt, he assured her that she was just feeling nervous, which was natural.

The entire exchange confused her. Based on research, the earlier the medication was started the better the outcome, so waiting until eight weeks seemed risky. Despite her insistence, he refused to prescribe her anything, sent her to get her blood drawn, and told her he would see her in two weeks. Leah asked if she could at least get an ultrasound to alleviate her anxiety because she was under the impression that six to eight weeks was recommended for the first scan. In her desperation to be heard, she even threw in the "geriatric pregnancy card." Again, he refused, saying it would not show anything yet.

One week later, Leah began spotting. She called her doctor's office, terrified that something horrible was happening. They assured her it was normal to spot during implantation (which should have already happened at that point). She begged to come in, and finally they relented. This time she brought her husband.

MEDICAL GASLIGHTING, WOMEN, AND YOUNG GIRLS

Medical gaslighting, which happens when healthcare providers downplay medical symptoms with non-medical opinions and emotional reasoning, is an example of societal gaslighting many women experience. In 2019, a survey conducted by the *Today Show* and SurveyMonkey showed that 17 percent of women felt they had been mistreated in healthcare as compared to 6 percent of men.

Unfortunately, preteen and teen girls experience medical gaslighting at a young age, as the stereotype of them being dramatic, overemotional, or promiscuous if they ask for contraception plays out in their healthcare treatment. While the Hippocratic Oath "first, do no harm" should include the self-esteem, self-worth, and emotional development of these young girls, often it does not.

According to the Guttmacher Institute, as of 2023, nine states permit individual healthcare providers to refuse services regarding contraception to women. This information is constantly changing, and the latest developments can be tracked on this state legislation tracker: guttmacher.org/state-policy. Rather than empower women and young girls to be the stewards of their own body, they must defer to someone else to make the decision for them. Taking bodily power away from women is a dangerous form of gaslighting. If medical practice and legislature deem women incapable of making sound choices for themselves, is this much different than labeling them "hysterical"?

Sitting in the office, Leah felt nervous and sick to her stomach. The doctor came in and sat down in the chair across from her. As he went over the results of the blood work, Leah noticed the doctor was speaking to her husband, which confused her because she was the one pregnant. The doctor asked her husband if *he* thought she should be prescribed progesterone, as if she was not even in the room. Her husband looked at Leah—unsure if he should speak for his normally headstrong wife—and then back at the doctor and agreed.

Leah and her husband left that day, prescription in hand, and a plan with the practice to monitor her thyroid levels going forward. While Leah was grateful that her pregnancy was still viable, she couldn't help but feel like her opinion had not mattered at all. It seemed to her she could have sent her husband to the appointment alone, even though she was the one carrying the baby.

CASE 2
"I Know My Child"

Natalia was a single parent to a beautiful little girl, Sophie. Her daughter, who had just started second grade, was biracial, bilingual, and very bright. Natalia described her as vibrant, talkative, and adventurous. The two of them were incredibly close and talked every night while snuggled in her daughter's bed. Natalia has been in therapy since her divorce, which was tumultuous and required a great deal of energy from her to continue parenting while working and going to business school.

Due to all the demands on Natalia, she was unable to volunteer at Sophie's school functions, but she still tried to show up for her when she could. She helped her daughter with homework and encouraged her growth and learning by planning special outings and opportunities for the two of them when she was not working.

One evening, they were cuddling before bedtime and her daughter said she did not want to go to school anymore. She had never said anything like that before. When Natalia pressed her daughter for more information, she refused and said she "didn't know why." The next day Natalia contacted the teacher to ask if there was anything going on in the classroom she should know about. The teacher said everything seemed fine to her.

A month passed and Sophie's resistance toward school evolved into stomach pain and headaches. Natalia recognized this as a sign of anxiety in children and contacted the guidance counselor. The counselor agreed to a meeting, but encouraged Natalia to meet first with her child's teacher before she became involved. Natalia agreed and set up a time to speak first with her daughter's teacher.

In the meeting, Natalia sat across from the teacher, who had been working in the school for several years. The teacher seemed warm and genuinely curious while asking Natalia about how things had been going at home. As Natalia answered her questions, she noticed they were not discussing anything happening at school. Natalia mentioned this, as well as her desire to figure out why her daughter had been struggling. The teacher's demeanor shifted, and she deflected back onto Natalia, *stereotyping* about how hard it must be to be a single mother.

Natalia was confused; why did her single parenting matter? Her daughter did not seem unhappy at home, the issue was when she was in school. The teacher went on to mention that "some kids have a more difficult time at school when their parents cannot be involved. I'm not sure if you know, but studies show that when parents are involved at school their children become more popular and confident with their peers."

Natalia was stunned. Had the teacher just *blamed her* for Sophie's issues in school? All her concerns had been ignored and thrown back at her. The rest of the meeting did not improve. That evening, Natalia emailed the guidance counselor to share her concerns. The next day, she received a response that supported the teacher and brought up her extensive experience working with kids "like Natalia's daughter." Natalia finally got it. She was beginning to understand that her own child, who was incredibly receptive and intuitive, was most likely feeling marginalized and stereotyped, just as she was. Her second grader did not have the language yet to describe what was happening. With few options, they finished the school year, but Natalia searched for a new job so they could move to another school district as soon as possible.

That next year, Sophie was enrolled at a new school that has been historically more inclusive and structured on values that aligned with their own. At the end of the first day of class, Natalia was relieved to see her daughter get off the bus with a huge smile on her face. She asked her daughter how school was, and her daughter replied, "I love my new school, Mommy. I can't wait to go back tomorrow."

CASE 3
"The Only Black Student"

Melanie always had a penchant for music. In high school, she played the drums and, when she contemplated where to go to college, she only had one university in mind, which was abroad in Toronto. Before this, we had been meeting for years to address family trauma and its impact on her anxiety. Her white mother was Canadian by birth and her father was African American. Melanie had said she always identified with both cultures and had travelled extensively due to her father's role in the military.

A few weeks into the start of her first year at the university, we met for a session, and she described an instance of covert gaslighting that left her questioning her decision to continue at her school. She had enrolled in a music history course and, while reviewing the curriculum, discovered a glaring omission of pretty much any music created by people of color. She noticed one week focused on classical jazz, but the remainder of the semester was music historically associated with white culture.

She explored her complex reaction to this in therapy, unsure what to do. The following week, her professor, a white male who had been teaching at the university for nearly 30 years, began his lecture on jazz. Looking around the classroom, Melanie noticed that not only was the professor white, but so was every other student. Her professor also seemed to take notice. As he spoke, he kept looking at Melanie. At one point, he asked the room if anyone had heard of a specific, influential jazz musician. When no one answered, he stopped in front of her seat and asked her directly, "What about you? Have you ever heard of him?" Her body tightened and she felt a wave of discomfort as she shook her head. He did not ask anyone else in the room and continued to launch through the lecture.

Melanie spent the rest of class feeling uncomfortable. It wasn't as if he was trying to treat her negatively or said anything bad about her race, yet it felt inappropriate. When class ended, she took her time gathering her materials and waited for the other students to leave the room. She approached her professor and asked, "Was there a reason you only asked me if I knew about the historically Black music?" He squinted at her, looking puzzled. She continued, "It just seems like you were singling me out, and I did not appreciate it." She exhaled deeply as she made her feelings known. Her professor paused for a moment, and she thought he may acknowledge her concerns, but instead he took a deep breath in and started laughing uncomfortably. He *denied* singling her out and lied, saying that he had called on other students. He said he saw all his students as the same—further acknowledging his discomfort with her race—and that accusations like that were not to be taken lightly.

Melanie felt confused. Hadn't she been the only one he called on? He then went on to tell her if she felt too uncomfortable in the classroom dynamic, she could drop the class. Instead of offering to adjust, acknowledge, or understand her, the professor lied and shifted the blame back on to Melanie, effectively accusing her of being the problem. He knew that she had no other choice but to take the class, as he was the only professor who taught the course required for her degree.

For the rest of the semester, Melanie was silent. She did not feel comfortable being the student she was, one who readily spoke up and felt confident about her ideas and the desire to share them. When she contemplated bringing the topic up to her advisor, she considered the entirely white music department and decided against it.

CASE 4
"The Publicist"

Lauren was 20 years into her career in public relations, dedicating her time and energy to the same company. She had risen to the position of account manager, which had her overseeing and managing the media image for a handful of large food distributors in the United States. When she was not busy putting out PR fires, she was also managing a team of professionals working at the same firm.

She put work high on the priority list in her life, as well as single handedly raising her two young daughters. She was eager to help, eager to please, and empathized for others both in her work and personal life. She sought out counseling to learn to prioritize herself, as well as processing family trauma and recovery from a broken marriage.

During one session, Lauren came into therapy markedly stressed and in tears. A client from one of her larger accounts was constantly evading bad press and again she had to pick up the pieces. This was her job and she was well equipped for it, but what she had not anticipated was the emotional abuse she would encounter while doing so. Part of dealing with the press is creating statements that are shared with large media outlets, and Lauren was particularly detailed in her research when drafting pieces.

When she sent the statement to her client for approval, he responded with an email veiled in anger, disgust, and venom. He demanded a phone call with her. She obliged, and when he got her on the phone he proceeded to call her "stupid" and accused her of fabricating the numbers she used in the report. He threatened her intelligence and integrity by using the *withholding* tactic, attempting to make her question if her report made any sense. Lauren was stunned. She had been painstaking in her research and put only the truth in the report. Instead of her client admitting he was terrified of the news getting out, he accused her of being the entire reason there was an issue in the first place, which was illogical, as she was only the messenger. He threatened to report her for defamation if she ran the story, and so she was stuck between his emotional manipulation and the truth. Tears streamed down her face as she remembered the self-doubt she felt in that moment.

After processing what happened, Lauren came to realize that the client was completely out of line for questioning her abilities, and that she did not deserve to be the target of his emotional manipulation. Despite her realization, she was concerned about what he would do to retaliate if she ran the full truth. She decided not to change the truth of the report but she did leave portions out. From there, she created a fortress around her, walling him out as much as possible while still remaining professional. She delegated his account to another person on her team and decided to involve herself only if necessary. She refocused on the many other facets of her job and remained as distant as possible.

SUMMARY & CONCLUSION
Teaching Those in Power to Listen

Power is often the motivation for gaslighting, and with societal gaslighting, this is no exception. As shown in the past four cases, when a person in power is charged with the well-being of others, they may be called upon to let go of their pride, status, and need for power in exchange for learning and growing. In all four cases, issues began when the women were not listened to. Their sources of information, persistence, sensitivity, identity, and personal experiences were questioned and trivialized.

In Stephen Covey's bestselling book *The Seven Habits of Highly Effective People,* he explores the power of listening. According to Covey, many of us are in the habit of listening to respond instead of listening to hear or understand the other person. The result is misunderstanding, conflict, and a lack of empathy, and leaves one person or group feeling unseen.

In cases of societal gaslighting, when there is misinformation or a lack of resources and/or research, those in charge would benefit from saying, "I don't know the answer; let me look into that," or "You know yourself better than anyone else, tell me more," and then deferring to the other person. This would demand that those in power are willing to share their power equitably. For medical care, the results could be improvements in research, knowledge, and options for women in the future. This also applies to racial gaslighting. BIPOC women being discriminated against and stereotyped rather than seen and understood perpetuates the problem. Stories, voices, and personal experiences need to be heard, not disregarded. Those in a place of authority need to carry both confidence about their knowledge and skills, as well as cultural humility. The remedy to societal gaslighting is a desire to learn more about what we do not know, and the ability to admit when we may be wrong.

STANDING UP TO SOCIETAL GASLIGHTING

Jennifer Ashton, ABC News's chief medical correspondent, explored the impact of medical gaslighting of women and people of color. She shared some important tips for what to do if you feel your doctor is disregarding your medical concerns.

- Keep a journal of symptoms, going back as far as possible to when the problem began.

- Ask the doctor, "What would you ask if you were a patient and experiencing these symptoms?

- Get a second or third opinion when possible.

While these tips apply to medical gaslighting, keeping records of your experience and seeking other's opinion of any situation—perhaps the HR department in a work setting or your advisor in an academic setting—can serve as protective factors for women who believe they are being gaslit.

PART TWO
HEALING

How you love yourself is how
you teach others to love you.

—RUPI KAUR, *MILK AND HONEY*

Part Two offers tools to promote healing; to increase mindfulness, self-compassion, self-regulation, and self-acceptance; to improve assertiveness; and to enhance boundary setting—all important components of healing from gaslighting and emotional abuse.

Recognition is the first stage of change, and Chapters 5 and 6 help you confront past trauma and emotional abuse. From there, Chapter 7 will identify unhealthy patterns that are keeping you stuck and will encourage change to promote healing and a greater sense of self.

As you progress through the chapters, you may find some of the exercises to be challenging. Slow down and take your time. Monitor how you feel and manage your expectations. Healing is a personal journey. Every individual is working at their own pace and timeline.

CHAPTER 5

Confront Past Traumas

This chapter will help you understand how relationship trauma can play a role in your life and overall health and well-being. Trauma may stem from childhood, crossing from one generation to the next, impacting attachment wounds such as struggling to trust others, or feeling comfortable expressing your needs. Because trauma impacts healthy attachment, this chapter also explores how to cope with current attachment patterns with the hope of having more secure relationships in the future. From there, you will learn how to integrate the knowledge learned into current and future relationships.

Large "T" Trauma versus Small "t" Trauma

A trauma response occurs when there is an inability to respond to a threatening event at the time it occurs. Whether a trauma event causes long-term issues depends on factors such as the ability to fight back or leave a situation, resilience, support, and whether the event causes long-term harm (for instance, loss of a loved one or independence). Too often, trauma that does not threaten physical safety is minimized as not being "traumatic." For both types of trauma, it is important to seek support and treatment—however, understanding what type of trauma has been experienced helps validate the impact these experiences can have and promotes recovery and healing. The following exercise identifies how trauma falls into two distinct categories: small "t" and large "T" traumas.

WHAT YOU'LL LEARN
- How to identify relationship trauma that is otherwise overlooked when discussing post-traumatic stress disorder (PTSD) and mental health
- The difference between small "t" and large "T" trauma

WHAT YOU'LL NEED
- 10 minutes when you feel relaxed and alert
- Memory of current and/or past traumas that disrupted your life

EXERCISE

Based on growing research, we are beginning to understand that trauma is more about the individual's perception of their experience rather than the event itself. Singular, extraordinary events that overwhelm someone's bodily sensations, beliefs, and thoughts, and are potentially life-threatening, are known as large "T" traumas. While large "T" may be easier to identify as being traumatic, it is not the only form of trauma. Simply being human makes us susceptible to small "t" trauma. Small "t" traumas do not involve violence or immediate disaster, but they cause distress by "1,000 papercuts."

Below you will find a checklist of both small "t" and large "T" trauma events you may have experienced. Acknowledging what you have endured and knowing how to label it can be a powerful part of the healing process.

Review both lists and place a checkmark next to any trauma you experienced. It is not necessary to remember any of the details surrounding your trauma (for example, if you were a young child and have only been told about the experience but do not recall any details), as trauma memories are stored in images and felt sensations in the body as opposed to a distinct story with a beginning, middle, and end.

SMALL "t" TRAUMA EXPERIENCES

_____ A breakup

_____ Death of a pet

_____ Losing a job

_____ Getting bullied

_____ Rejection from a friend group

_____ Moving

_____ Non-life-threatening injuries

_____ Emotional abuse

_____ Being marginalized

_____ Gaslighting

LARGE "T" TRAUMA EXPERIENCES

_____ Rape/assault

_____ Natural disasters

_____ Homelessness

_____ Witnessing loss of life

_____ Death of a loved one

_____ Physical abuse

_____ Childhood abuse/neglect

_____ War

_____ Violent crimes

_____ Serious car accident

_____ Medical trauma

With small "t" traumas, the effect worsens over time and exposure. The more stressed someone is, the more these traumas impact their resilience (the ability to cope with difficult things). Practicing resilience skills, such as expressing your feelings about these traumas, reduces their negative impact.

With large "T" traumas, the effect worsens if the individual is not able to "fight back" or "do something" about the trauma. While trauma symptoms are common within the first month for all survivors, symptoms that persist after three months and interfere with daily life and/or relationships may be a sign of PTSD. In such a case, it is beneficial to reach out to a medical provider for further support and assessment.

ACE Test for Childhood Trauma

WHAT YOU'LL LEARN

- What kind of impact childhood trauma can have on future health outcomes
- How healing tools can increase resilience, helping mitigate the impact of an adverse childhood

WHAT YOU'LL NEED

- 10 minutes when you feel relaxed and alert
- Memory of some (but not necessarily all) childhood events
- Journal (optional)

With over 17,000 original participants, the ACE study (1995–1997) was one of the largest investigations of childhood trauma and it still informs the treatment of trauma and its impact on health to this day. Many clinicians and researchers make use of the scale to help assess the level of trauma and risk factors in those they are working with. The survey tallies different types of abuse, neglect, and other hallmarks of a difficult childhood and has been found to accurately predict correlations between the presence of these adverse childhood experiences with physical and mental health problems later in life.

Your ACE score does not holistically predict your future, but instead can be used as guidance. The scale does not take your current lifestyle into account, meaning you have a great deal of power over your future health outcomes.

EXERCISE

The ACE Scale

While you were growing up, before the age of 18:

1. Did a parent or other adult in the household often or very often . . . a) Swear at you, insult you, put you down, or humiliate you? or b) Act in a way that made you afraid that you might be physically hurt?

   If yes, enter 1 ____

2. Did a parent or other adult in the household often or very often . . . a) Push, grab, slap, or throw something at you? or b) Ever hit you so hard that you had marks or were injured?

    If yes, enter 1 _____

3. Did an adult or person at least 5 years older than you ever . . . a) Touch or fondle you, or have you touch their body in a sexual way? or b) Attempt or actually have oral, anal, or vaginal intercourse with you?

    If yes, enter 1 _____

4. Did you often or very often feel that . . . a) No one in your family loved you or thought you were important or special? or b) Your family didn't look out for each other, feel close to each other, or support each other?

    If yes, enter 1 _____

5. Did you often or very often feel that . . . a) You didn't have enough to eat, had to wear dirty clothes, and had no one to protect you? or b) Your parents were too drunk or high to take care of you or take you to the doctor if you needed it?

    If yes, enter 1 _____

6. Were your parents ever separated or divorced?

    If yes, enter 1 _____

7. Was your mother or stepmother . . . a) Often or very often pushed, grabbed, slapped, or had something thrown at her? or b) Sometimes, often, or very often kicked, bitten, hit with a fist, or hit with something hard? or c) Ever repeatedly hit at least a few minutes or threatened with a gun or knife?

    If yes, enter 1 _____

8. Did you live with anyone who was a problem drinker or alcoholic, or who used street drugs?

   If yes, enter 1 _____

9. Was a household member depressed or mentally ill, or did a household member attempt suicide?

   If yes, enter 1 _____

10. Did a household member go to prison?

    If yes, enter 1 _____

    Now, add up your "Yes" answers: _____
    This is your ACE Score.

Score interpretation: If the ACE score is 1–3 without other health conditions (such as severe allergies or asthma), there is "intermediate risk" for toxic stress. If the ACE score is 1–3 with at least one ACE-associated condition, or if the ACE score is 4 or higher, there is "high risk" for toxic stress (which can lead to further physical or mental health issues).

Identifying your ACE score can feel difficult, as it is a concrete depiction of past trauma. It is important to remember that the scale does not account for efforts made to improve your health, and anything done to increase resilience can have a positive impact on mental and physical well-being. Being aware of your ACE score can act as a motivator to help you become a cycle breaker if you choose to practice validation and self-compassion by recognizing what you overcame.

Are You Dealing with a Trauma Bond?

According to the *National Domestic Violence Hotline*, it can take survivors upwards of seven times to leave their aggressor successfully. At the center of the issues lies a trauma bond, which is a fundamental part of the cycle of abuse. The cycle of abuse includes four stages: tensions building, explosion/abuse, reconciliation/ repair, honeymoon/calm (see image on page 37).

Trauma bonds exist in all types of relationships and are difficult to detect because the repair efforts made through love bombing often overshadow the negative aspects of the relationship. Understanding what a trauma bond looks like is essential for making healthy relationship choices and knowing when to end an unhealthy relationship.

WHAT YOU'LL LEARN
- Why trauma bonds form and how they are maintained
- How to identify the classic signs and characteristics of a trauma bond

WHAT YOU'LL NEED
- 10 minutes when you feel relaxed and alert
- A memory of a relationship that caused concern

EXERCISE

The following questions represent common characteristics and emotions experienced in a trauma bond. Take your time to release yourself from self-blame and to practice self-compassion by providing honest answers. Place a check mark next to your answer.

1. Do you find yourself alternating between loving and missing the other person and feeling intense anger towards them for what they have done to you?

   Yes, at least some of the time _____
   No, never _____

2. Do you ever feel that you owe the other person for something they have done for you, even though they mistreat you? (For example, have they paid for your home, schooling, car, or health insurance, or taken care of other financial needs?)

   Yes, at least some of the time _____
   No, never _____

3. Do you find yourself feeling responsible for helping the other person grow and become a better version of themselves? And, if so, do you feel anger or guilt if you do not succeed?

   Yes, at least some of the time _____
   No, never _____

4. Are you ever made to feel like you are responsible for the other person's well-being and worry what will happen to them if you leave the relationship?

   Yes, at least some of the time _____
   No, never _____

5. Do you find yourself covering up for the other person's unhealthy behavior by making excuses or minimizing?

   Yes, at least some of the time _____
   No, never _____

6. Do you feel you have to "walk on eggshells" around the other person to keep them happy or to maintain peace?

   Yes, at least some of the time _____
   No, never _____

7. Do you ever question if you deserved negative feedback or treatment because of something you have done in the present or past?

   Yes, at least some of the time _____
   No, never _____

8. Are you often made to feel guilty?

   Yes, at least some of the time _____
   No, never _____

9. Have you ever imagined leaving or tried to leave the relationship and were unsuccessful due to fear of any kind (such as fear of abandonment, financial stress, being alone, or what others will think)?

   Yes, at least some of the time _____
   No, never _____

10. Do you feel frequently controlled by the other person (physically, emotionally, sexually, spiritually, or financially)?

    Yes, at least some of the time _____
    No, never _____

If you answered yes to three or more items, you are likely dealing with a trauma bond. Though the severity of these dynamics varies in each relationship, even one item can signify a potential trauma bond, causing an imbalance of safety or power.

How Trauma Impacts Attachment

WHAT YOU'LL LEARN
- The four primary attachment styles
- How trauma can impact our attachment style
- The characteristics of secure attachment so you know how to become more securely attached

WHAT YOU'LL NEED
- 15 minutes when you feel relaxed and alert
- Reflection of how you function in relationships
- Pen and paper

Attachment theory was first developed in the 1950s by John Bowlby and later expanded on by Mary Ainsworth. Ainsworth, who primarily focused on mother-child attachment, described healthy attachment as a "secure base in which to explore." The foundation of attachment theory is that the goal of the human infant is to maintain closeness with its caregiver. In *Anxiously Attached: Becoming More Secure in Life and Love*, couples counselor Jessica Baum states that in relationships where we can be our "real" selves, "we are able to access even deeper states of being and discover the joy of being accepted for who we truly are." In adulthood, this translates to getting needs met in our relationships. Examples of secure attachment include expressing your emotions by asking for what you want and need, setting boundaries, and choosing trustworthy people to spend time with. Developing a more secure attachment leads to more independence and authenticity, as there is less fear of abandonment.

Being aware of your style can help you navigate current and future relationships. Bowlby identified four types of attachment styles: **secure, anxious-ambivalent, disorganized, and avoidant.**

Secure attachment appears as being expressive and trusting with needs and emotions, while also being capable of autonomy for both you and the other person.

The **three "insecure" attachment styles** that trauma can cause include:

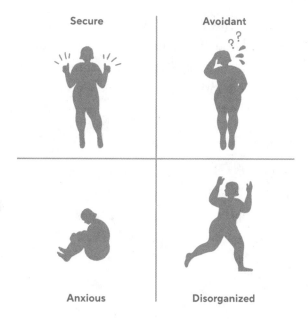

Secure · Avoidant · Anxious · Disorganized

- **Avoidant attachment,** which can appear as being distant or dismissive. There may also be anxiety when approached with intimacy or vulnerability.

- **Anxious attachment** appears as being preoccupied with the state of the relationship and the intentions or feelings of the other person. This constant state of anxiety can appear as ambivalence when feeling overwhelmed by obsessive thinking and worry.

- **Disorganized attachment** is common after experiencing interpersonal, complex trauma and appears as a fearful or avoidant reaction to intimacy, while also fearing abandonment.

When a child's needs are not met, they adjust their behavior to reestablish closeness, even if the method is not personally beneficial. Let's look at an example with a child whose caregiver is highly critical. If the child feels upset or insecure around their caregiver, they would be less likely to share their feelings, out of fear of being judged as "unlovable." As a result, the child will act as if they do not care what their caregiver thinks and, in turn, become avoidant when they feel strong emotions or insecurity. In adulthood, this translates to not wanting to get close in relationships out of fear of being judged, or pushing people away who do want to be close. Romantically, it may look like a person who is only interested in someone who is dismissive or "plays hard-to-get."

EXERCISE

The following are the top 10 traits for each of the four attachment styles. Reflect upon your past and present relationships and place a check next to those that most apply to you from each category. After completing the checklist, tally the total number of checks for each style. The style with the most marks aligns most with the style you may be operating in.

SECURE

_____ Comfortable in a close relationship

_____ Able to depend on partner and vice versa during times of need

_____ Accepts partner's need for separateness without feeling rejected or threatened

_____ Can be close and independent ("dependent–independent")

_____ Trusting, empathic, tolerant of differences

_____ Forgiving

_____ Communicates emotions and needs openly

_____ Attuned to partner's needs and responds appropriately

_____ Remains present when in conflict

_____ Able to manage emotions concerning relationship issues

Total _____

AVOIDANT

_____ Emotionally distant and rejects intimacy; keeps partner at arm's length

_____ Partner always wants more closeness than you can give

_____ Equates intimacy with loss of independence; prefers autonomy to togetherness

_____ Unable to depend on partner or allow partner to "lean on" them

_____ Communication is intellectual, uncomfortable when talking about emotions

_____ Avoids conflict altogether or is explosive

_____ Narrow emotional range (cool, controlled, stoic)

_____ Prefers alone time

_____ Good in a crisis; non-emotional

_____ Takes charge

Total _____

ANXIOUS-AMBIVALENT

_____ Insecure in intimate relationships; worried about rejection and abandonment

_____ Preoccupied with relationships

_____ Needy; requires ongoing reassurance and/or close connecting with partner

_____ Unresolved past issues consistently impact present perceptions of relationships

_____ Highly sensitive to partner's mood/actions; takes partner's behavior personally

_____ Highly emotional and at times argumentative, combative, angry, and controlling

_____ Poor personal boundaries

_____ Communication is not collaborative but rather self-protective

_____ Deflects blame if feeling insecure

_____ Unpredictable and moody; connects through conflict

Total _____

DISORGANIZED

____ Unsettled mindset and emotions about unresolved past traumas

____ Difficulty tolerating emotional closeness in relationships

____ Argumentative

____ Difficulty regulating emotions

____ Recreates past relationship patterns by being abusive and dysfunctional

____ Has intrusive trauma memories and triggers

____ Dissociates during conflict to avoid pain

____ Antisocial; struggles with empathy and remorse

____ Aggressive and punitive

____ Focused on own needs first out of fear of being hurt

Total ____

KEEP IN MIND

- Attachment is not a state trait (which are characteristic patterns of thinking, feeling, and behaving that generalize across most situations); rather, it is a learned response pattern formed as a result of past relationships that can also be impacted by current ones. This means there is always potential to work towards secure attachment within safe relationships.

- While disorganized and insecure patterns develop because of traumatic relationships in the past, our brains have the capacity to rewire due to neuroplasticity, or the brain's ability to change through growth and reorganization. Like a groove in a record, what is repeated becomes more present, whether it is a belief, habit, new learned skill, or, in this case, an attachment style.

- According to Stanford professor and researcher Andrew Huberman, we can reinforce positive neural networks by increasing focus around a new behavior and then following the focused behavior with sleep or rest in the form of meditation through Non-Sleep Deep Rest (NSDR).

- Different relationships may illicit different attachment styles to emerge. For example, if you have a healthy relationship where you feel safe, you may express yourself more (secure attachment). In contrast, if you are around a gaslighter who minimizes your feelings and shifts blame when they are wrong, the most common *defense style* will emerge. In the face of conflict, the style that kept you safe in the past will become most present in a toxic relationship.

- Our defense style may also surface in healthy relationships any time we feel threatened or triggered. It is beneficial to share your attachment style with the other person and engage in dialogue when you feel reactive (for instance, telling your partner that you may push them away if you feel smothered. You can ask for space in a healthy way that does not project blame onto the other person).

- In Amir Levine and Rachel Heller's groundbreaking book *Attached: The New Science of Adult Attachment and How It Can Help You Find—and Keep—Love,* they caution that certain attachment styles are not as compatible, particularly anxious paired with avoidant. These two styles have contradictory traits that can be highly triggering to the other. When triggered, both partners can feel unsafe and remain activated, making it hard to establish a stable, secure, and trusting connection.

Subjective Units of Distress Scale (SUDS)

WHAT YOU'LL LEARN

- Common physical symptoms associated with distress and trauma response
- How to use the Subjective Units of Distress Scale (SUDS) to increase awareness and resilience in times of stress

WHAT YOU'LL NEED

- 10 minutes when you feel relaxed and alert
- The SUDS Scale template from the exercise
- Pen and paper

Feeling unsafe or dysregulated is detrimental to those in recovery from trauma. Because trauma is stored in the body, the body is much more sensitive to stress after experiencing trauma. Physical trauma symptoms can arise from triggers that, at times, appear random. Understanding that there is an end to a trauma response is a powerful way to cope when symptoms arise.

One way to measure trauma response is with the Subjective Units of Distress Scale (SUDS), created in the 1950s by psychiatrist Joseph Wolphe. SUDS is a self-report scale ranging from 0 to 10 measuring subjective intensity of disturbance or distress currently experienced by an individual. SUDS can help determine how intense a trauma response is while providing insight into which triggers elicit stronger distress in the body. In my own practice, I recommend that any client experiencing distress of 4 or above use a grounding or coping strategy. Anything above 7 may need more intense intervention or outside support.

EXERCISE

Use the SUDS thermometer below to help visualize your personal sub-jective units of distress. This differs for everyone; something that may be highly triggering for one person will differ greatly for another. For this exercise, begin at 0 and identify what feeling or experience you would associate with that SUD (for example, 0 may be meditating or napping). As you move up the scale be mindful not to "jump" to extremes too quickly. For example, conflict with a co-worker may seem like a 70 but when thinking of other, more intense experiences (such as loss of a loved one) you might decide to lessen the SUD for the previous example. This is normal and part of learning more about our individual SUDS. Especially for those who have experienced trauma, distress tolerance is negatively impacted and things that may seem like they should be rated at a lower level (such as being late to work) can elicit a more intense response than anticipated.

When creating your scale, be kind, gentle, and curious about the process. If it becomes difficult, complete the confidence building and self-love practices found in Chapters 8 and 9 and then come back to this exercise.

PHYSICAL SIGNS OF DISTRESS (AND COMMON PHYSICAL TRAUMA RESPONSES) INCLUDE:

- Sweating

- Pounding heart, feeling shaky

- Rapid or irregular breathing and/or the inability to inhale deeply

- Physical agitation (pacing, clenched jaw, tense muscles)

- Upset stomach/lack of appetite

- Confusion and/or dissociation from physical self and surroundings

- Exhaustion

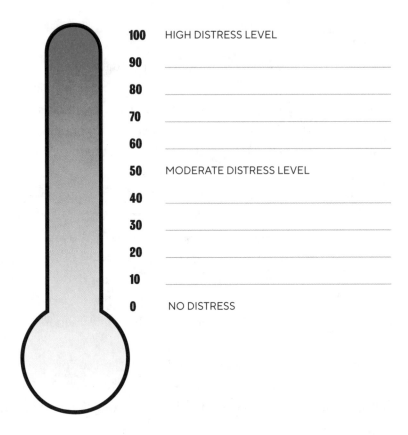

100 HIGH DISTRESS LEVEL

90 _____

80 _____

70 _____

60 _____

50 MODERATE DISTRESS LEVEL

40 _____

30 _____

20 _____

10 _____

0 NO DISTRESS

Now that you have completed your personal SUD scale, you can use this as a reference for future stressful situations. Ask yourself: *What is my SUD score in this moment?* If you feel you are approaching 40 percent, utilize a coping strategy as soon as possible. Strategies can be breathwork, mental grounding tools (like counting backwards from 10 or noticing visual characteristics of the space around you), releasing physical tension through movement (such as push-ups, going for a walk, splashing cool water on your face, or dancing), or resting. Intervening at lower levels, even below 40, is an excellent way to manage stress, staving off potential trauma triggers before they occur.

Remember, *no feeling is final*, which is also true about general stress. Paying attention to when your distress lessens (as evidenced by a lower score on the SUDS) helps you recognize that there is a beginning, middle, and end to stress.

BRINGING IT ALL TOGETHER

As quoted from Resmaa Menakem, "Trauma in a person, decontextualized over time, looks like personality. Trauma in a family, decontextualized over time, looks like family traits. Trauma in a people, decontextualized over time, looks like a culture."

As women, we are tasked with so much responsibility in our relationships, and too often we forget that the relationship with ourselves is just as, if not more, important. Acknowledging what triggers a trauma response for you by exploring your current or past stressors and traumas is a powerful way to gain insight into your current relationships, mental health, and sense of self. While it can be difficult to reflect on the past, recognizing what you have endured and overcome can help rebuild your future and validate your experience. This is especially important when a gaslighter questions, minimizes, or trivializes your past.

As Menakem explains—we are not our trauma, but rather are those who experienced it. To expand his quote for women, I would say: Trauma in women, decontextualized over time, looks like a gender.

CHAPTER 6

Stand Up for Your Emotions

Gaslighting is a form of emotional abuse intended to break you down, but this chapter will help build you up. The tools described within will empower you to stand up for yourself, set healthy boundaries, and reclaim what you want and deserve. You'll also learn effective conflict resolution and ways to assert yourself in the face of gaslighting. By acknowledging your experience with gaslighting, this chapter also provides valuable insights to identify and stop gaslighting in its tracks.

Identifying Forms of Emotional Abuse

Emotional abuse includes all attempts to control, isolate, or emotionally manipulate, threaten, or instill fear in the victim. Some forms of emotional abuse may seem obvious, while others are more subtle signs that develop over time. Emotional abuse is not physical; rather, its intention is to cause harm to the thoughts and feelings of another. Being able to detect when you are experiencing emotional abuse is a powerful way to protect yourself from its harmful effects.

EXERCISE

In this exercise, you will be asked to reflect on your own potential experience with emotional abuse in a relationship. (Feel free to repeat this exercise exploring other relationships, if necessary.) There are four categories: **humiliating-criticizing, control-shame, accusing-blaming, neglect-isolation**. Each category provides a brief description of potential motivating factors and a number of examples for that specific form of emotional abuse.

- Writing directly in the book, circle any forms of emotional abuse you may have experienced in your current or past relationship.

  or

- Choose to list any tactics you have experienced on a separate sheet of paper suffered.

- Identify how many you have experienced in each category.

WHAT YOU'LL LEARN
- How to identify various forms of emotional abuse
- How to decipher between healthy and abusive expression

WHAT YOU'LL NEED
- 10 minutes when you feel relaxed and alert
- A memory of current or past relationships to reflect on
- Pen and paper

HUMILIATING-CRITICIZING

These tactics attack self-esteem and self-worth. Examples include:

- name-calling and derogatory nicknames
- character assassination
- bringing up old mistakes
- focusing on your failures
- yelling
- belittling
- public embarrassment
- dismissiveness
- joking at your expense
- insulting your appearance
- making fun of your interests

CONTROL-SHAME

These tactics intend to gain and maintain power and control while instilling a feeling of inadequacy. Methods of control may include:

- making threats to harm you or someone you love
- monitoring your whereabouts
- spying on you digitally
- gaslighting
- making all the decisions
- controlling your finances
- weaponizing guilt
- constant lecturing
- ordering you around
- frequent, unwarranted outbursts
- feigning helplessness
- unpredictability
- walking out or threatening to leave
- stonewalling (shutting you out and ignoring you)

ACCUSING-BLAMING

This tactic intends to elevate the abuser above their target, sustaining a hierarchy with them in power. Examples might include:

- unfounded jealousy
- weaponizing guilt
- extreme expectations of perfectionism from their partner
- blaming you for being too sensitive
- denying the abuse
- trivializing your feelings
- blaming you for their problems
- purposefully creating issues and denying doing so

NEGLECT-ISOLATION

This tactic includes isolating you from your support network so you prioritize their needs and neglect your own. Tactics may include:

- refusing eye contact
- keeping you from socializing
- invalidating your boundaries
- coming between you and your family
- using the silent treatment
- withholding affection
- shutting down any communication
- working to turn others against you
- denying you support and demoralizing you if you need it
- interrupting what you are doing if you are not attending to them
- devaluing your feelings

After identifying the examples of abuse that you have experienced, answer the prompts below:

The person or relationship I am reflecting on is:

_____

_____

The ways this person emotionally abused me were:

_____

_____

What I feel now about this abuse:

_____

_____

If you choose, you can end with this statement:

I recognize this experience as emotional abuse and I deserve to seek support, help, or safety if necessary.

If you fear immediate physical violence, get to a safe place if you can. You can also call 911 or your local emergency services for help.

If you aren't in immediate danger but feel you need to talk to someone, you can call the 24/7 National Domestic Violence Hotline at 800-799-7233 to find resources for service providers and shelters across the United States.

Identifying Potential Codependency Patterns

Awareness is a brave first step toward self-empowerment, making it less likely for codependency patterns to persist. This tool helps increase awareness of problematic patterns that are common when struggling with codependency.

The term codependency describes an intense and unhealthy connection to another person—often coming at the expense of one's own needs and wellness. While this is part of the equation, it is not the full scope of the issue. When someone suffers from low self-esteem because of manipulation from gaslighting and emotional abuse, they are at a greater risk for codependency. They are also more likely to neglect their own needs and prioritize others, causing harmful codependent patterns that can become personally damaging.

Codependency is not always negative, as there *are* relationships where heightened codependency is healthy, for example mother–baby, but, as we grow, it is healthy to develop individuality. When a codependent relationship prevents self-empowerment, the result is harmful to our self-esteem, mental health, and even physical health.

Identifying a codependent relationship or personal codependency patterns can be difficult to accept. Clients of mine have expressed being "embarrassed" by their behavior. Remember that codependency doesn't define you; rather, it is a set of *coping skills* that develop from unhealthy relationships and environments.

WHAT YOU'LL LEARN
- How gaslighting and emotional abuse cause codependency
- Typical patterns of codependency
- Support resources for codependency

WHAT YOU'LL NEED
- 20 minutes when you feel relaxed and alert
- Pen and paper

EXERCISE

The comprehensive checklist in the sidebar comes directly from Co-Dependents Anonymous (CoDA.org), founded in the 1980s as "a fellowship of people whose common purpose is to develop healthy and loving relationships." It is a tool given to new members of the 12-step group as a means for self-exploration and discovery.

After reviewing the list, highlight the traits you identify with and/or create a list using a separate piece of paper. If you identify a pattern that closely describes you and your experiences, you may want to explore further resources at CoDA.org.

Once you identify your potential patterns, it can help to receive support from others who have had similar experiences. CoDA.org is a wonderful resource for learning further information on the topic, as well as finding both virtual and in-person groups for recovering from codependency.

PATTERNS AND CHARACTERISTICS OF CODEPENDENCE

The following lists are offered as tools to aid in self-evaluation and may be particularly helpful to newcomers as they begin to understand codependency. These lists may aid those who have been in recovery for a while to determine what traits still need attention and transformation.

Denial Patterns
Codependents often

- have difficulty identifying what they are feeling.
- minimize, alter, or deny how they truly feel.
- perceive themselves as completely unselfish and dedicated to the well-being of others.
- lack empathy for the feelings and needs of others.
- label others with their negative traits.
- think they can take care of themselves without any help from others.
- mask pain in various ways, such as anger, humor, or isolation.
- express negativity or aggression in indirect and passive ways.
- do not recognize the unavailability of those people to whom they are attracted.

Low Self-Esteem Patterns
Codependents often

- have difficulty making decisions.
- judge what they think, say, or do harshly, as never good enough.
- are embarrassed to receive recognition, praise, or gifts.
- value others' approval of their thinking, feelings, and behavior over their own.
- do not perceive themselves as lovable or worthwhile.
- seek recognition and praise to overcome feeling less than.
- have difficulty admitting a mistake.
- need to appear to be right in the eyes of others and may even lie to look good.
- are unable to identify or ask for what they need and want.
- perceive themselves as superior to others.

- look to others to provide their sense of safety.
- have difficulty getting started, meeting deadlines, and completing projects.
- have trouble setting healthy priorities and boundaries.

Compliance Patterns
Codependents often

- are extremely loyal, remaining in harmful situations too long.
- compromise their own values and integrity to avoid rejection or anger.
- put aside their own interests in order to do what others want.
- are hypervigilant regarding the feelings of others and take on those feelings.
- are afraid to express their beliefs, opinions, and feelings when they differ from those of others.
- accept sexual attention when they want love.
- make decisions without regard to the consequences.
- give up their truth to gain the approval of others or to avoid change.

Control Patterns
Codependents often

- believe people are incapable of taking care of themselves.
- attempt to convince others what to think, do, or feel.
- freely offer advice and direction without being asked.
- become resentful when others decline their help or reject their advice.
- lavish gifts and favors on those they want to influence.
- use sexual attention to gain approval and acceptance.
- have to feel needed in order to have a relationship with others.
- demand that their needs be met by others.
- use charm and charisma to convince others of their capacity to be caring and compassionate.
- use blame and shame to exploit others emotionally.
- refuse to cooperate, compromise, or negotiate.
- adopt an attitude of indifference, helplessness, authority, or rage to manipulate outcomes.

- use recovery jargon in an attempt to control the behavior of others.
- pretend to agree with others to get what they want.

Avoidance Patterns

Codependents often

- act in ways that invite others to reject, shame, or express anger toward them.
- judge harshly what others think, say, or do.
- avoid emotional, physical, or sexual intimacy as a way to maintain distance.
- allow addictions to people, places, and things to distract them from achieving intimacy in relationships.
- use indirect or evasive communication to avoid conflict or confrontation.
- diminish their capacity to have healthy relationships by declining to use the tools of recovery.
- suppress their feelings or needs to avoid feeling vulnerable.
- pull people toward them, but when others get close, push them away.
- refuse to give up their self-will to avoid surrendering to a power greater than themselves.
- believe displays of emotion are a sign of weakness.
- withhold expressions of appreciation.

DEAR MAN for Conflict Resolution

WHAT YOU'LL LEARN
- How to feel more confident in the face of conflict
- How to use the dialectical behavior therapy (DBT) interpersonal effectiveness skill DEAR MAN to establish and maintain assertiveness while reaching conflict resolution

WHAT YOU'LL NEED
- 15 minutes when you feel relaxed and alert
- A current or past conflict to use for the exercise
- Pen and paper

Confidence during conflict resolution is crucial when dealing with gaslighting, as a gaslighter wants their target to be influenceable, allowing the gaslighter to manipulate their target more easily. DEAR MAN is a dialectical behavior therapy (DBT) skill, developed by psychologist Marsha M. Linehan, that helps with being tactfully disagreeable while still maintaining a healthy connection with the other person in the face of intense emotions and conflict. This skill provides a frame-work for being assertive and asking for what you want, while also maintaining your message—regardless of the response from the other person.

EXERCISE

After reading the DEAR MAN sample and guide, choose a personal conflict (past or present) and create your own DEAR MAN statement.

SAMPLE CONFLICT

You have a friend who is constantly cancelling plans at the last minute.

Describe: I notice you cancelled our plans the last three times we were going to hang out.

Express: It makes me feel frustrated.

Assert: I would prefer you wait to commit until you are sure you can hang out.

Reinforce: I bet this way we will see each other more, which would be fun.

Mindful: I will breathe slowly while I speak.

Appear Confident: I will make sure I do not speak too softly.

Negotiate: I will tell her I am fine with her cancelling at least two days before so I can make other plans.

DEAR MAN

Describe the situation and stick to the facts.
Use observations such as "I notice," "I see," or "I hear," supplemented with specifics about the situation, without adding too much detail that can derail you.

Express your feelings using an "I" statement.
Be careful not to use feelings as accusations, such as "I feel you are being disrespectful." Rather, use "I feel disrespected."

Assert means to ask directly for what you want or say "no" very clearly.
For example: "I would like" or "can you please."

Reinforce the positives that can come out of the person listening, changing, or at least understanding where you are coming from.

Mindful: Remain mindful of how you feel in the moment.
If you feel distracted, come back to your breath, and notice your surroundings. If the other person is defensive, try keeping the conversation on course.

Appear Confident: Regardless of how you feel internally, it is helpful to appear confident by using eye contact, open body language, and a clear tone of voice (see "Power Posing," page 127).

Negotiate: Be willing to hear the other person's point of view and when possible, adjust your request and negotiate. (Unless the other person is emotionally abusive or gaslighting you.)

YOUR CONFLICT

_____

_____

Describe: _____

Express: _____

Assert: _____

Reinforce: _____

Mindful: _____

Appear Confident: _____

Negotiate: _____

KEEP IN MIND

- Being assertive is not being aggressive. DEAR MAN is much more effective when it is _clear_ rather than aggressive.

- Not everyone will agree, respond well, or respect a DEAR MAN statement. If this happens, stay firm in your boundary or request by using the "broken record method," which involves reaffirming your request or boundary by repeating the DEAR MAN statement again. Remaining mindful and firm in your request makes it less likely someone can manipulate your emotions, thus making you less susceptible to the effects of gaslighting. If the other person gaslights you, make efforts to disengage from the conflict.

- DEAR MAN may feel scripted when you are first practicing, but the more often you try the skill, the more natural it will become.

- It is not necessary to follow the acronym in order. For instance, if you "Express" before you "Describe," that is fine—just make sure to hit all points when you can.

Boundary Setting for Women

When setting boundaries, it is helpful to recognize the way it makes you feel. Commonly, "unearned guilt," which is feeling guilty for something you are not responsible for, is associated with boundary setting. For a victim of gaslighting, it can seem like you have done something wrong by setting a boundary, but in fact the opposite is true. Boundary setting is beneficial for the health of a relationship, as it prevents resentment while increasing healthy intimacy.

EXERCISE

To begin, identify physical sensations and thoughts you have associated with boundary setting.

When boundary setting my body feels: *(tense, stressed, sweaty, etc.)*

_____

_____

_____

_____

_____

WHAT YOU'LL LEARN
- How to use "no" as a full sentence
- The importance of boundary setting in the face of emotional abuse
- Common "go-to" phrases to help set boundaries effectively

WHAT YOU'LL NEED
- 15 minutes when you feel relaxed and alert
- Pen and paper

Thoughts or ideas I associate with boundary setting include:

_____

_____

_____

_____

_____

_____

The following are common phrases for boundary setting, using language that expresses either a firm or a flexible boundary.

These flexible boundary statements acknowledge the other person's opinion and allows for ongoing conversation. Flexible does not mean you are going to back down, but rather it is an open tone used when asserting yourself.

- "I respect your opinion, but I have my own as well."

- "I am sorry, but I don't have time."

- "That is not going to work for me."

- "Let me pause you right there."

- "I appreciate your advice, but I am going to try something else."

- "While I cannot do _____, I am willing to do _____."

- "We see things differently."

- "It's okay if you do not agree or understand how I feel."

- "While I would like to say yes, I've overcommitted and am unable to do this."

- "I would like for you to respect my boundary."

Here are common firm boundary statements. These are used when someone has previously disregarded your boundaries or is disrespecting the boundaries you are sharing now. These firm statements are most effective with a clear, but mindful tone.

- "I don't have time."

- "I don't want to."

- "No." *(This is a full sentence and needs no further explanation!)*

- "That is not going to work for me."

- "I disagree."

- "I will not."

- "Please stop."

- "I will not change my mind."

- "I am not talking about this anymore."

- "I am not able to do this."

After reading both flexible and firm boundary statements, choose a conflict from your past or present where you need to set boundaries. In the space below, write what the conflict is and then write your chosen boundary setting phrase:

_____

_____

_____

_____

_____

_____

KEEP IN MIND

It does not always feel good to set boundaries, especially if you are unaccustomed to doing so. Practice first with people you consider safe to increase your tolerance for boundary setting. I once had a client who started by simply asking for "paper over plastic." She was afraid to upset anyone she knew personally in her life, so she decided to start with the cashier at the grocery store. A seemingly small boundary catapulted her into practicing boundary setting in progressively more challenging situations and relationships in her life. Every boundary set is a form of self-love and self-empowerment that is worth celebrating!

Emotional Individuation versus Agreeability

The following tool provides a crucial skill for recovering from emotional abuse and gaslighting by practicing *emotional individuation*—the ability to achieve an independent identity from others. Agreeable people are often warm, friendly, and tactful; however, being *too* agreeable can be a trauma response called *fawning.* In his book *Complex PTSD: From Surviving to Thriving*, author and therapist Pete Walker defines fawning as the act of someone trying to become more appealing to others by people-pleasing or avoiding conflict to sustain a sense of safety. Perpetual fawning can lead to issues with codependency. When a gaslighter makes their love and acceptance conditional on their victim being agreeable, it erodes emotional individuation because having an opposing opinion usually leads to issues and strain in the relationship with a gaslighter. When gaslighters attack their victim's identity, it includes their inner voice, and emotional individuality is one way to claim it back.

WHAT YOU'LL LEARN

- What emotional individuation is, why it is important, and how to practice it
- How constant agreeability can cause issues with codependency
- How to achieve independence and strengthen your identity

WHAT YOU'LL NEED

- 10 minutes when you feel relaxed and alert
- Pen and paper

EXERCISE

Poor emotional individuation makes it more likely that you will rely on other's opinions to form your own. There are eight billion people with different opinions in the world; it's impossible to please everyone and for everyone to agree with you. Having your own opinion is healthy, sexy, empowering, exciting, and completely your right as a woman.

To put this concept into practice, take a moment to remember simple things about yourself that make you unique. Fill out the following lists to get to "re-know" yourself by remembering what you like and don't like.

WHAT ARE YOUR FAVORITES?

Foods: _____

Movies: _____

Music: _____

Places to vacation: _____

Colors: _____

Other favorite things: _____

_____

_____

WHAT ARE YOUR DISLIKES?

Pet peeves: _____

Foods: _____

Music: _____

Colors: _____

Vacation destinations: _____

Other things you dislike: _____

_____

_____

Next, reflect on a time when you felt you could not express your opinion. Think about what you would have said to the other person (or group of people) if you felt there were no consequences:

_____

_____

_____

_____

_____

Continuing Your Emotional Individuation Practice

Here are a couple of ideas to help you continue strengthening your emotional individuation.

- When someone asks for your preference, (where would you like to eat, what movie would you like to watch, etc.) take a moment to think of an answer, even if you feel ambivalent at the time. This person is inviting you to practice this skill.

- If someone who is safe expresses an opinion you do not agree with, take a deep breath, and remind yourself that your opinion is valuable and that it is safe to share it.

- Assess your current relationships for whether you feel safe expressing yourself. Determine if those are relationships you want to focus your energy on.

- Remember that repetition is key. Some of us were trained to be "agreeable" from a very young age, and it can be a difficult habit to correct. The more experience you have practicing this, the more natural it becomes.

In working with a self-proclaimed "people pleaser," we created this mantra:

I am not everyone's cup of tea

To stop caring what people think of you is nearly impossible. We are human, and we want to be accepted by the tribe. Instead you can make a decision to replace this desire with a different thinking pattern, a personal mantra. Feel free to try mine on for size.

Fact Tracking

Gaslighters may make you feel like a "bad person" for being disagreeable or having your own opinion. They may even highlight the concept that you are "bad" or "wrong" and they are "good" or "right" to make you doubt yourself further. This is a common manipulation tactic of gaslighting, intended to erode your sense of reality. The good thing is, there is a way to counter gaslighting with *fact tracking*. The following tool will provide a space to remind yourself of what you have experienced, as well as a blueprint for setting necessary boundaries going forward.

EXERCISE

Fact tracking is a useful practice to combat gaslighting that may include saving texts, emails, voicemails, or even journaling about things the gaslighter said or did that made you uncomfortable or feel unsure. The intention is not to share the information with the gaslighter, as they may weaponize it against you, but, rather, to help you sustain your sense of reality. There may be times, however, when gathered information would be used in a legal case or when reporting the gaslighting to a support person or authority figure (for example, human resources, if the gaslighting occurred in the workplace). It is imperative to remember that fact tracking is a healthy, normal, and helpful way to check back on what has happened to you by helping you regain clarity about gaslighting you have experienced.

WHAT YOU'LL LEARN

- Specific methods for re-examining or keeping track of gaslighting tactics used against you
- How to reaffirm your memory and experiences
- A method to gather information in the case of legal necessity

WHAT YOU'LL NEED

- 15 minutes when you feel relaxed and alert
- Pen and paper

In the table below, you will find a fact tracking guide that asks important questions for past reflection. If necessary, review Chapter 1, Gaslighting Tactics (page 13).

POTENTIAL GASLIGHTING BEHAVIORS	DATE OF INCIDENT	WHAT OCCURRED?
Denial		
Withholding		
Trivializing		
Diverting		
Countering		
Stereotyping		
Deflection		

MEANS OF COMMUNICATION (I.E., TEXT, CALL)	EMOTIONS SURROUNDING THE EVENT	DID YOU REACH OUT TO A SUPPORT PERSON? IF SO, WHO?

To expand on this table, use the space below to include any further incidents you would like to record:

_____

_____

_____

_____

Choose a date you will review your fact-tracking exercises to remind yourself of your experiences:

_____

_____

_____

If you feel comfortable doing so, choose a safe support person to share your exercise with:

_____

_____

_____

_____

Finally, remember that what happened is real and how you feel is real and the gaslighter is the last source of reality you need concerning what happened. Their sense of reality is only what serves them best, and most of the time what benefits them is not the truth.

BRINGING IT ALL TOGETHER

One of the common misconceptions about emotional abuse is that it is less harmful than physical abuse, but the reality is that our brains do not decipher between emotional and physical pain. Research shows that psychological pain fires similar areas of the brain as physical pain, meaning emotional abuse from gaslighting can cause harm as much as physical abuse. These experiences impact our ability to stand up for ourselves, which is why this chapter focused so much on building your sense of self and individuality.

Remember that your opinion matters. You have a right to say no, and it is healthy to set boundaries. It is your right to be disagreeable. No one can possibly please everyone—there are simply too many people in the world. Being an "emotional chameleon" occurs when you are in a constant state of changing who you are and how you feel to adjust to other people's preferences or personalities, which increases the risk of being targeted by potential gaslighters.

Clients often ask me questions about assertiveness: "When is the best time to set boundaries?" "Is it ever too early in a relationship to be direct with what I want?" or "How early in a relationship can I start to say no?" The answer to each of these is "As soon as possible." The sooner you express what you need, the more likely you will "weed out" potential abusers. This can feel scary for those who struggle with *rejection sensitivity* or the fear of abandonment, but once a negative relationship ends, there truly is more space for healthier ones. Standing up for yourself can feel like a huge risk, but it is a remarkably healthy one. As a therapist, I champion healthy risk-taking with my clients, and I would like to champion this for you as well.

CHAPTER 7

Break Unhealthy Patterns and Get Unstuck

Gaslighting can cause feelings of confusion and powerlessness, leading to unhealthy patterns that paralyze you in various areas of life. The good news is that there are ways to break these patterns by using powerful focus strategies to improve motivation and lead to successful goal setting. This chapter offers meditation, self-compassion building, and focus strategies to help quiet the inner critic, ensuring that you will be successful in what you truly care about.

Focus Meditation

A study from NYU researching exercise motivation found that participants who focused on the finish line were able to outperform those who were told not to look at the end goal. Not only did looking at the finish line improve motivation, but it increased perception of performance (confidence). The following tool integrates principles from this research by using values-based goal setting (creating goals based on what values matter most to you) with the power of meditation, helping you to increase focus on your goals and improve confidence in achieving them.

WHAT YOU'LL LEARN
- How to shut out external distractions (noise) and refocus on your end goal

WHAT YOU'LL NEED
- 5 minutes of uninterrupted time
- Private space
- Pen and paper

EXERCISE

The following are seven common values associated with life satisfaction. Reflecting on what feels most important to you, rank them from 1 to 7 (with 1 being the most important and 7 being least).

_____ Romantic relationships

_____ Financial security

_____ Knowledge

_____ Creativity

_____ Spirituality

_____ Health

_____ Family

Examine your top three values and select one you would like to work towards improving.

_____

_____

_____

_____

Identify one long-term goal related to that value. For example, if you rated creativity as an important value in which you feel stuck, you might set a goal to join an art class. It can be helpful to create a SMART goal that is Specific, Measurable, Attainable, Relevant and Time bound. (For example, "I will attend one 60-minute art class by the end of this month.")

Write your goal below:

_____

_____

_____

_____

Next, you will meditate on this goal.

- Set a timer for 5 minutes (or longer if you wish).

- Find a relaxed position either sitting or lying down. If you are sitting, make sure your feet are flat on the ground. Elongate your spine and make any final adjustments necessary.

- Close your eyes (or, if you prefer, find a soft gaze in front of you), relax the muscles in your face and take a slow deep inhale to the count of 4, hold for 4 and exhale for 4, letting go of tension in your body. Continue this style of breathing (also known as box breath) for at least 5 cycles.

- Allow your breath to settle into a natural rhythm.

- Now, imagine what it would look like to accomplish the goal you set in as much detail as possible and while engaging your five senses (For example, visualize walking into the art class, smelling paint, and feeling the warmth of the sun streaming through the windows).

- When distractions arise, such as thoughts about self-doubt, time, money, or responsibilities, simply notice them with gentle curiosity.

- Rather than removing distractions, refocus on the image of accomplishing your goal in as much detail as you can.

- Repeat this practice of refocusing on your goal as much as necessary.

- End with one box breath cycle and gently open your eyes.

Use this space to journal about your meditation experience and anything you felt or discovered during the exercise.

_____

_____

_____

_____

_____

_____

_____

_____

_____

_____

Making Change with Compassionate Self-Talk

WHAT YOU'LL LEARN
- How compassionate self-talk can help you get unstuck
- How positive reinforcement through self-compassion can reverse the negative effects of gaslighting

WHAT YOU'LL NEED
- 15 minutes when you feel relaxed and alert
- Pen and paper

Practicing self-compassion is a crucial part of making positive change after experiencing gaslighting. Dr. Kristen Neff, a leading psychologist, professor, and author, defines self-compassion as "being warm and understanding toward ourselves when we suffer, fail, or feel inadequate, rather than ignoring our pain or flagellating ourselves with self-criticism." She proposes that we "speak to ourselves the way we would speak to a friend." Science supports this idea, as research shows that we are less likely to learn a new skill when we feel criticized. The following exercise identifies how negative self-talk is holding you back, while also encouraging a kinder, more compassionate inner voice.

EXERCISE

Think of a time when you felt frustrated or disappointed in yourself. What types of things did you say in those moments to "motivate" yourself or correct your behavior?

The first box has been filled in with a sample. Fill in the rest of the boxes with other self-talk statements you have used.

CURRENT MESSAGING
I am horrible at getting things done.

When reading your current messaging, how do you feel about yourself and your ability to meet your goals?

_____

_____

_____

_____

In the next section, you will reframe how you speak to yourself. For each statement you used in Current Messaging, reframe each phrase to how you would speak to a friend or someone you care about. Some of your statements may already have a compassionate tone—that is excellent! If that's you, simply add more kind options in the chart below. The first one again has been completed as an example.

REFRAMING WITH COMPASSIONATE SELF-TALK
I am really busy and overwhelmed, making it hard to get everything done.

When reading the compassionate self-talk messages, how do you feel about yourself and your ability to meet your goals?

_____

_____

_____

_____

KEEP IN MIND

- Gaslighting can increase the inner critical voice as you wrestle with negative messaging from the gaslighter. Critical self-talk can become habitual, making it feel impossible to break unhealthy patterns and meet goals that will bring you more joy.

- Change is more likely with encouragement rather than criticism. The more often you use compassionate self-talk, the more likely change will happen.

- In addition to changing *what* you say, it can help to change *how* you say it. Tone of voice and nonverbal communication are equally if not more important than the words we choose. I once had a client who would critically yell at herself "Breathe!" while at work and struggling with adult ADHD. After completing this exercise, she decided to say the same thing with a gentler tone, and her old negative phrase became a soothing grounding tool for her.

Capsule Choices

WHAT YOU'LL LEARN
- What decision fatigue is and why it may be keeping you stuck
- The power of capsule choices to manage stress and prevent the onset of decision fatigue

WHAT YOU'LL NEED
- 15 minutes when you feel relaxed and alert
- Pen and paper

The stress of recovering from gaslighting is depleting, but couple that with the 35,000 decisions adults make daily and you get decision fatigue. Also called *ego depletion*, a term coined by psychologist Roy F. Baumeister, decision fatigue happens when we are "tapped out" from making choices and we either become impulsive or shut down (for instance, eating healthy all day and then eating only junk at night). Our decision stamina increases in one of two ways: rest (in the form of sleep or meditation) or eating. Every decision made uses glucose to create energy in the brain, so eating and/or resting restores the energy needed for making future choices.

EXERCISE

The following exercise helps reduce the number of decisions made daily, which is especially important when you are busy or experiencing high levels of stress. By using capsule choices to reduce the number of options for any given decision, you learn to reduce unnecessary decisions, giving you more stamina to make healthy choices on your healing journey.

A commonly known capsule choice is the "capsule wardrobe," where you keep a limited number of interchangeable clothing items in your closet to make a variety of outfits. This practice reduces the clutter both in your closet and in your mind. Another common option is food. According to research done at Cornell University, we make an average of 227 choices daily on food alone.

Limiting meal choices at times you are busy or feel depleted is an excellent way to reduce decision fatigue.

The following are common choices you can "capsulize." Check any categories that you would like to try to capsulize and identify up to three options (or more, if necessary) for that category. There are also three blank categories to add any of your own ideas. Feel free to use the table below or prepare a separate journal if you would like to expand on this exercise.

CATEGORY	YES/NO	CAPSULE CHOICES
Meal ideas		
Clothing options (i.e., what you will typically wear to work)		
Ways to relax		
Support people to call		
Self-care routines for stress		
"Go-to" physical activity during the work week		
"Go-to" physical activity on the weekend		
Music to listen to		
Friends to spend time with		
Healthy snacks if tired/ depleted/stressed		

KEEP IN MIND

- Some capsule choices work better during the work week while others apply more to the weekend. It can help to create different "go-to" choices for both. (For example, a smoothie or salad for lunch at the office, but perhaps more spontaneity and variety on the weekend.)

- This exercise not only helps to capsulize self-care and decision-making, but it is also a wonderful exercise when getting to know yourself as you heal from the effects of gaslighting.

- Pre-planning by using capsule choices also helps to increase will-power when trying to form healthy habits. By reducing the options, you are less likely to make impulsive choices when you are depleted.

Habit-Forming Plan: Using Tips and Tricks from Experts in the Field

Many of us struggle to maintain healthy habits to help us feel our best. Especially after gaslighting, it can be difficult to focus on your goals because so much energy went into making sure the gaslighter was happy. Now it is your turn to focus solely on yourself. This exercise will use the power of behavioral psychology to help you succeed at a personal goal by teaching you habit-forming strategies tested over time by experts in the field.

EXERCISE

First, identify a goal that will help you thrive during your recovery journey from gaslighting (Example: I want to make meditation a regular habit).

My goal:

_____

_____

Next is an overview of some of the most effective strategies for achieving your goal. Give yourself time to read through each concept, allowing for reflection on how to apply these strategies to your own life.

WHAT YOU'LL LEARN
- How to positively impact your environment to form new habits
- How to prioritize repetition to change your brain and make new habits easier to maintain

WHAT YOU'LL NEED
- 20 minutes when you feel relaxed and alert
- A personal goal
- Pen and paper

HABIT-FORMING STRATEGIES FROM EXPERTS IN THE FIELD

- **Mini goals versus grand goals.** James Clear, author of the best-selling book *Atomic Habits*, explored what experts in the field say about effective habit forming and found that small goals are often the essential steps needed toward achieving an ultimate goal. For example, if your goal is to run a 5K, mini goals would be to run 5 times per week for 15 minutes. This helps create a habit and provides the positive feedback of success, which can be built upon for larger goals.

- **One percent more effort every day = large yearly return.** Research shows that it takes very little effort to reach a goal, as long as it happens regularly in small increments. Mathematically speaking, if someone were to strive for 1 percent improvement each day, then, by the end of the year, they'd be over 31 percent better than where they were at the start of the year.

- **Four percent difficulty is key!** If something is not challenging *enough*, we lose motivation but if it is *too* difficult we are likely to give up. The magic number is to attempt something that is 4 percent more difficult than you are currently capable of. This also supports the idea of mini goals over time for a big reward.

- **Monitoring is essential for all types.** Based on author Gretchen Rubin's concept of the Four Tendencies, we fall into separate categories for motivation and change. You can take her quiz online at gretchenrubin.com/quiz/the-four-tendencies-quiz and discover if you are an *obliger*, *upholder*, *questioner*, or *rebel*. From there, she explores how to set goals and make changes using your unique tendency. If we try to set goals outside our tendency, it is remarkably more difficult. For example, if you are an obliger and you want to start a running routine, you will be more likely to succeed if you are "obliged" to meet up with a running buddy and are accountable to someone else. However, if you are a rebel you may feel resistant to being told when and how to run and you'd be more likely to succeed if you did so on your own terms and when the mood strikes.

- **Accountability buddy.** Even if you are not an obliger, most of us need some form of accountability. This may look like choosing a person to report your progress to, someone who will attempt the goal with you, or simply someone to "body double" for you, an ADHD coping strategy where someone is physically present to help improve focus while the other person attempts a challenging task.

- **Pointing-and-calling your habits.** Because awareness is crucial for making change, finding a method to literally point to and/or say our habit out loud can be very helpful. This simple trick raises our consciousness. Think back to decision fatigue—when we are stressed or tired, we may not even be aware of some of the choices we make that prevent growth. One excellent resource for this is the "Habits Scorecard" that James Clear also shares on his website at jamesclear.com/habits-scorecard.

- **Novelty is useful so the first time is a charm.** Ever notice how a dessert tastes better on the first bite, or how we tend to set goals that start on a Monday? There is a reason for this and it has to do with our brain's reward centers. When something is novel, we receive more feel-good hormones like dopamine and serotonin as a result. Using this as a guide, it really does help to set goals at the start of something, such as a new school year, or by investing in novel items to help with our goal. So if your goal is to journal, it may actually help to purchase a brand-new journal to start writing in.

- **Know if you are an abstainer or a moderator.** In Gretchen Rubin's book *Better Than Before*, she explores beyond the four tendencies to study personality traits that impact habit formation. When comparing abstaining versus moderating, some people truly need to abstain altogether from something—for instance, going "cold turkey" from smoking cigarettes—while others benefit from the intermittent reward of cutting back and practicing "harm reduction" when breaking a habit. An example of someone who may benefit from tapering off a habit would be a rebel who may buck against the strict nature of abstaining and need to lean into change. Figuring out which type you are can help you get unstuck and move forward with goals.

- **Reframe goals in the positive as opposed to negative.** Based on the widely acclaimed book *The Secret,* you can use the law of attraction for goal setting. Instead of stating what you do not want, state what you do want. When we state what we do not want (carrying massive debt, for instance), we narrow our focus on the negative, which limits creativity. Instead, reframing thoughts to the positive (finding a job that pays well), your whole focus reorients and your inner dialogue is more likely to have a positive tone. An example I often give my clients is the idea of riding a bike. If I tell you to ride the bike straight but stare at a tree to your right, no matter how hard you try—unless you are an acrobat—your bike will drift toward what you are focused on. You must keep your aim on what you want and not what you don't want.

Using the "Habit Forming Plan" below, journal about how you can apply each of these strategies to your previously set goal. These questions can also be used for reflecting on setting future goals by helping you master change, growth, and healing in the future.

What mini goals can I set?

_____

_____

_____

_____

_____

What will my 1 percent more effort daily look like? How will I know I am making progress?

_____

_____

_____

_____

_____

What would make this goal too easy and how can I make it at least a 4 percent challenge?

_____

_____

_____

_____

_____

Upon taking the Four Tendencies quiz, or from self-reflection, which tendency am I and how can I apply that to my goal?

_____

_____

_____

_____

_____

Who will I be accountable to? (This can be a helping professional, a coach, or someone running a program you sign up for, or even an objective friend knowledgeable in what my goal entails.)

_____

_____

_____

_____

How will I track or "point out" my habits?

_____

_____

_____

_____

How can I use novelty to help me with my goal?

_____

_____

_____

_____

Do I plan to abstain or use moderation?

_____

_____

_____

_____

_____

How can I describe my goal using positive phrasing? What is it I _do_ want?

_____

_____

_____

_____

_____

Using the **Habit Forming Plan**, explore your original goal from page 110. How can you revisit this goal after learning more about habit forming? Using a SMART goal format, rewrite your strategy informed goal below.

_____

_____

_____

_____

_____

BRINGING IT ALL TOGETHER

Gaslighters often attack the very things that empower women to gain power and control over them. As a result, women who survive gaslighting can struggle with prioritizing themselves, which negatively impacts their self-confidence and self-esteem. This was seen in the relationship between Sarah and Jill in Chapter 3. Jill pressured Sarah to not participate in her passion of rock climbing, taking away empowerment and individuality from Sarah. When recovering from gaslighting, focus on what is important to you by setting healthy goals and getting unstuck. Experiencing a sense of accomplishment helps strengthen your self-esteem and confidence with a positive feedback loop. By doing so, you are creating a story that you are capable of anything. This sense of confidence and connection with your inner voice makes it easier to identify gaslighting and stand up for yourself in the face of it.

How to Stay Motivated

This chapter explored the power of meditation, positive self-talk, and coping with decision fatigue, as well as other tips and tricks for goal setting. Because goal achievement is unique for everyone, it is helpful to choose skills that most resonate for you, and once you discover them—stick with what works. Even the planning stage of creating a new habit can be empowering, because focusing on your goals and how you plan to achieve them creates hope for healing and change.

As you move forward in this book, you will learn self-care strategies to help you thrive, find joy, and improve your confidence. Come back to this chapter if you ever feel stuck when trying to form new, healthy habits for healing after gaslighting. To set your intentions for the next part of this book, take a moment to create a Vision List for what you hope to achieve.

Mel Robbins, author and motivational speaker, cautions not to only envision your end goals, but also some of the tricky steps along the way. A simple goal such as *meditate for five minutes per day* can be a powerful step towards your big dreams.

MY VISION LIST

As I move into the next part of this book and think of myself thriving,
I envision achieving these goals.

1. _____

_____

_____

2. _____

_____

_____

3 _____

_____

_____

4. _____

_____

_____

5. _____

_____

_____

PART THREE
THRIVING

Do your thing and
don't care if they like it.

—TINA FEY, *BOSSYPANTS*

Part Three focuses on thriving after gaslighting abuse. Tools in this section come from integrative therapies backed by research focused on women's well-being. You will learn skills to cultivate thriving by increasing self-esteem and confidence, while encouraging a growth mindset. You will learn ways to practice self-love and embrace who you truly are. The final chapter offers actionable ways to learn how to trust others again and build healthy relationships in the future. As you focus on resilience practices to help you thrive, be patient with your progress, as healing is neither straightforward nor linear. Putting the skills to practice regularly will promote healing, but there can also be setbacks. All of this is normal. Remember to be kind to yourself during your healing journey.

CHAPTER 8

Build Up Self-Esteem and Confidence

Gaslighting can eradicate our sense of self, and rebuilding self-esteem is crucial to heal and thrive after an abusive experience. In this chapter, you will learn how to express your needs, increase your confidence, and know what you are truly capable of. Skills will focus on spending quality time with yourself, taking care of your body, tapping into the power of your breath, connecting with gratitude, and finding meaning in your personal story. Self-esteem and confidence built in this chapter are foundational for the future chapters where you will learn to practice self-love, discover more about who you truly are, and find comfort in trusting others again.

Dating Yourself

Women recovering from gaslighting often struggle with "knowing who they are" or even "liking themselves." This is truly difficult because the way a gaslighter treats you does not reflect the individual you truly are, and further distorts your self-image. "Dating yourself" is a beautiful way to work through these issues by helping to rebuild self-esteem as you dedicate your time, money, energy, and care inwards. When you focus more energy on loving yourself, you also increase your self-value. Some women may feel they are "faking it" when they do not feel authentic self-worth as a result of the impact of gaslighting, but consistency helps to change doubt and negative self-talk to self-awareness and self-love. As social psychologist and researcher Amy Cuddy says, "Fake it until you become it." The following exercise helps generate ideas and a plan for making "dating yourself" a personal commitment.

WHAT YOU'LL LEARN
- Creative ways to "date" yourself and how this can promote healing
- Ways to use self-care and self-compassion to get to know yourself again

WHAT YOU'LL NEED
- 10 minutes for planning
- Pen and paper

EXERCISE

The chart below provides eight focus areas for dating yourself. Gary Chapman's *The Five Love Languages*, heralded as being a blueprint for how we give and receive love, was used in creating this template. Each box has activity ideas to choose from and a space for you to fill in your own ideas. Feel free to either circle ideas that appeal to you or create a separate list. When dating yourself, you will have the opportunity to practice these efforts of self-devotion!

SELF-REFLECTION	PHYSICAL CARE
• Journaling • Vlogging • Horoscope exploration or astrology • Art therapy (e.g., self-portrait)	• Exercise • Alternative healing (e.g., acupuncture) • Get enough sleep • Research and take helpful supplements
GIFT-GIVING	**TRYING SOMETHING NEW**
• Splurge on something for yourself • Buy a new book • Buy yourself flowers • Purchase a spa gift card to use at a time you need it	• Create a list of hobbies you have wanted to try and do one • Learn a new language • Travel somewhere new • Find new music you may like
BOUNDARY SETTING	**WORDS OF AFFIRMATION**
• Practice the power of saying no • Limit unnecessary commitments • Distance yourself from unhealthy relationships • Stop saying "I hope you understand." You do not have to justify a boundary	• Start a gratitude journal • Practice compassionate self-talk • Compliment yourself • Share your accomplishments with those who support you

QUALITY TIME	PHYSICAL TOUCH
• Set aside alone time	• EFT tapping (see page 155)
• Turn a movie off if you do not like it	• Dry brushing (Ayurvedic practice)
• Meditation	• Use electric massagers
• Light a candle for yourself at dinner to create ambiance	• Seek out massages, facials, and other forms of physical self-care from caring professionals
• Take a slow walk on a beautiful day, perhaps listening to a book or music, or simply enjoying the silence around you	

PUTTING YOUR "SELF-DATING" ROUTINE INTO ACTION

• **Time Commitment:** Just like any relationship, the relationship with yourself requires consistent attention. Women tend to spread themselves thin with relationships, responsibilities, and commitments. Identify how much alone time you need to feel balanced, with a minimum of one "self-dating" practice occurring daily. Many highly sensitive people (HSPs) thrive from having at least two hours per day to themselves. This may not be feasible, but it is a healthy benchmark to consider.

• **Plan for Obstacles:** You can date yourself and practice self-love even when you are limited on time. Imagine a busy, hectic day. You cannot possibly fit one more thing in, but you *can* choose to speak to yourself kindly and perhaps practice intentional breathing for 60 seconds. Every moment counts.

• **Remain Curious:** Think of dating yourself as a constant learning experience. The more curious you are about yourself, the more you learn and the better your self-esteem will become. Journaling what you learn about yourself can be a powerful tool for deeper reflection.

Breath Practices for Thriving and Wellness

WHAT YOU'LL LEARN
- How breathwork can connect you with yourself in the here and now
- Two research-supported breath exercises to aid your healing journey after gaslighting abuse

WHAT YOU'LL NEED
- 5 minutes for each breath exercise
- A quiet space
- Pen and paper

I cannot breathe in the past, I cannot breathe in the future, I can only breathe in the present.

—*Unknown*

Our breath is one of the most powerful tools we have for reducing stress, improving our mood, and encouraging a sense of calm in the present. Learning skills to improve our breath is extremely important when recovering from gaslighting and emotional abuse. Stress, age, and life experience can disconnect us from the curative factors of healthy breathing and regularly practicing good breath hygiene helps to improve breath quality, as well as the ability to regulate stress. Not only are breathing techniques important *when* we are stressed but also *before.*

The more often breathing skills are practiced (preferably daily), the sooner we can recognize when we are stressed. The following are two research-supported breath skills that will support the healing process after gaslighting abuse.

EXERCISE

Box Breath

The first breath technique is highly accessible and easy to implement. According to reviews of research done at the Mayo Clinic, box breathing has been shown to lower blood pressure, reduce pain, stimulate brain growth, reduce anxiety and panic, improve sleep, and reduce the perception of overall stress levels. On his podcast *The Huberman Lab*, American neuroscientist and Stanford professor Andrew Huberman shares that box breathing has the capacity to retrain us to engage in a healthier breath pattern that includes not over-breathing (too rapid or shallow) and with the necessary pause between breaths when we are relaxed. The result is better carbon dioxide tolerance, which helps the body adapt to stress.

HOW TO DO BOX BREATHING

1. Find a comfortable position where you can easily expand your lungs (perhaps sitting up straight or lying down flat on your back).

2. Exhale slowly, emptying the air out of your lungs.

3. Slowly inhale through your nose as you slowly count to four in your head.

4. Hold (retain) your breath with your mouth closed to the count of four.

5. Slowly exhale to the count of four. (Some people tend to exhale too quickly. Learning to control your exhale is a powerful way to increase a sense of calm.)

6. Hold your breath for four counts, noticing the silence as you neither breath in nor out.

7. Repeat for four more rounds.

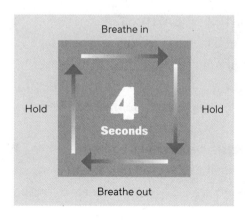

VARIATIONS AND CONSIDERATIONS

- One full cycle of box breath can be a powerful grounding tool if you do not have the time or ability to perform 5 full cycles.

- A variation that stimulates your vagus nerve—signaling "safety" in your body—is to hum on your exhale. This is a powerful tool for clearing your mind, similar to another breathing skill called "Bee's Breath," which you may also wish to explore during your healing journey.

- If you have practiced breathwork before or find you have a heightened carbon dioxide tolerance—as measured by how long it takes for you to comfortably empty your lungs—you may want to extend the time beyond four counts.

- Closing your eyes and paying attention to your body, feeling tension release, or witnessing sensations that arise can further amplify the benefits of this practice.

- Never forget how important the exhale is (slowing it lowers your heart rate) for anxiety and panic. Too often, we inhale quickly in the face of stress (which increases our heart rate). When experiencing a panic attack, we tend to take quick, shallow inhales. Balancing our inhale and exhale with box breathing helps to reduce the prevalence of these often-terrifying panic attacks.

ALTERNATE NOSTRIL BREATHING

The next technique is a yogic breath practice known as *Nadi Shodhana Pranayama* (Pranayama meaning "breath" in Sanskrit). The name means "subtle energy clearing" and when performed it has the potential for increasing the feeling of positivity in the body. Research has shown that this technique helps reduce anxiety, increases our sense of well-being, and relaxes the physical and mental body. In her book *What Happened*, Hillary Clinton wrote that she used this breath technique to cope with her presidential campaign loss. Further research on the benefits of this

Yogic breath found that it helps increase well-being in abuse survivors by balancing their autonomic nervous system, lowering stress, and improving overall mental health.

HOW TO DO ALTERNATE NOSTRIL BREATHING

1. Using the thumb of the right hand, close the right nostril and gently inhale, filling your lungs as much as possible. (You may choose to count your inhale to the count of 5 and exhale out to the count of 7, always trying to achieve a longer exhale. However, feel free to inhale and exhale as long as it feels comfortable, always trying to empty your lungs completely on the exhale.)

2. Next close the left nostril using your index finger and exhale completely through the right nostril.

3. Then, inhale through the right nostril.

4. Close the right nostril and breathe out through the left.

5. Continue this practice, alternating for each inhale and exhale (which is one breath cycle) for up to 5 minutes.

6. If you would like to use your left hand instead, simply reverse the instructions.

VARIATIONS AND CONSIDERATIONS FOR ALTERNATIVE NOSTRIL BREATHING

- If plugging your nose does not feel comfortable (for instance, if you are suffering from allergies or a cold), you can also opt to practice *Nadi shodhana*, which involves focusing your breath from one nostril to the next without plugging your nostrils. It is more of an "imagined" focus, but it can still stimulate your brain positively.

- If you start to feel lightheaded, dizzy, or nauseous, discontinue the breath practice and return to your natural breathing pattern. This is a normal part of learning how to expand your breath but be patient and kind to yourself and do not push too hard. The more you practice, the less likely these adverse effects will arise.

- Even if you do not have 5 minutes to perform this technique, only one cycle can help. Clients of mine have reported using one cycle as a grounding skill in the face of stress, a way to end a hot shower, or to help them drift off to sleep at night.

Power Posing

Power posing was made popular by Amy Cuddy's Ted Talk, "Your body language may shape who you are." This skill includes standing in a posture of confidence—even at times when you are unsure of yourself—and has been found to help people feel more powerful when attempting difficult tasks. Early findings by Cuddy and her fellow researchers suggested that holding a power pose for two minutes not only helped their study participants perform better on mock job interviews, but it also produced a favorable hormonal response for performance, with an increase in testosterone and decrease in cortisol (the stress hormone).

Since publication, there has been strong debate in the research community as to whether power posing produces the hormonal changes it promised; however, the improvement in perceived self-esteem and confidence is still supported. This self-improvement life hack is a useful confidence booster to have in your toolbox for thriving after gaslighting abuse. It is easy to implement and has the potential to send positive messaging to your brain while helping you mindfully connect with your body.

WHAT YOU'LL LEARN
- The science behind "power posing" and how to use it to increase your confidence and presence
- Ideas for when power posing can work to increase confidence and self-esteem

WHAT YOU'LL NEED
- 10 minutes when you feel relaxed and alert
- A mirror (optional)
- Pen and paper

EXERCISE

Write down an upcoming or past situation where you want or wanted to feel more confident (examples include a job interview or presentation, confronting someone about an issue, or trying a new skill).

_____

_____

_____

_____

On a scale of 1 to 10 (with 10 being most confident), rate how confident you feel about handling this situation.

_____

In the diagram on the following page, you'll find both "high" and "low" power poses. Take a moment to move through each pose to simply feel them in your body.

Once you get a feel for each pose, choose the high power pose that seems the most natural for you. Assume this position in a private space where you feel comfortable. (You can opt to practice an assertive gaze by standing in front of a mirror; this is completely optional and not necessary for practicing this skill.) Hold the posture for at least 2 minutes. To enhance the exercise, try connecting with your breath and remain mindful of judgments that may arise. If and when they do, notice them, and let them go.

After the 2 minutes, re-rate how confident you feel about the situation on a scale of 1 to 10 (with 10 being most confident).

_____

High Power Pose

Standing, wide stance

Arms raised in a V above the head

Hands on hips

Arms crossed behind the head, sitting or standing

Low Power Pose

Sitting with hands folded in the lap

Arms crossed over the chest

One arm across the body in a self-hug

Hunching

WHEN TO USE POWER POSING

- Any time you wish to embody power and presence is a good time to use power posing.

- This skill can also be done sitting down (for instance in your car if you are about to go into an interview) and is as much about your body as your state of mind.

- Power posing can also be used in the moment when talking or interacting with someone. The other person will likely detect if you keep an open and expansive stance, creating a positive feedback loop about your confidence.

- Power posing can help you become more grounded in your body amid a conflict. Try using it in conjunction with DEAR MAN.

- When making a speech or presentation, use power posing to gain confidence and quiet any stress you may be feeling.

In the space below, journal about times when you may want to use power posing.

_____

_____

_____

_____

_____

_____

_____

Wisdom Gratitude Practice

Feeling stuck in a negative thinking pattern is common after experiencing gaslighting. The "power of positive thinking" has been widely credited to improve mental health; however, it is difficult to know how to be positive when negative thoughts play on a repeat loop. Brené Brown, widely acclaimed author and researcher, describes gratitude as the opposing force to anxiety, fear, and depression. Meeting your negative emotions and fears with a deliberate practice of gratitude is an important part of healing. Practicing a gratitude mindset has a positive impact on processing trauma, as it has the potential to widen our perspective of past experiences. This does not mean we become grateful for the trauma itself, rather we are more capable of recognizing our personal growth and wisdom that comes from it.

WHAT YOU'LL LEARN
- How to find meaning from past trauma to cultivate healing
- How gratitude can change your perspective, improve mental health, and enhance overall well-being

WHAT YOU'LL NEED
- 10 minutes when you feel relaxed and alert
- Pen and paper

EXERCISE

This gratitude building skill is offered in two parts: Laying the Groundwork with Regular Practice followed by Wisdom Gratitude Practice.

Laying the Groundwork with Regular Practice

When recovering from gaslighting, establishing a regular practice of gratitude may feel unnatural or forced, but the more you practice the more comfortable and natural it becomes.

- Using a journal, notepad, or note-taking app on your phone, write down at least 3 things you are grateful for.

- Nothing is trivial (I am grateful for the almond milk decaf latte I had while writing this tool). The important thing here is not the significance of what you are grateful for, but rather the positive impact gratitude can have on your brain, body, and spirit.

- Practice daily. The goal is to make gratitude habitual by taking time to think of things to write, leading to thoughts of gratitude throughout the day, helping to increased resilience.

- After writing your list of 3 things you're grateful for, you can move to *Wisdom Gratitude Practice* immediately, or you can practice gratitude journaling for a week and then move to the next practice.

Wisdom Gratitude Practice

In your journal or the space below, write down something difficult that has happened to you (perhaps associated with your experience of gaslighting).

_____

_____

_____

_____

_____

How has this event impacted you?

_____

_____

_____

_____

_____

What sensations do you notice in your body when you think of this
experience?

_____

_____

_____

_____

_____

What would you do differently now because of this experience?

_____

_____

_____

_____

_____

When you focus on what you learned, what sensations or thoughts do you notice in your body?

_____

_____

_____

_____

_____

What, if anything, are you "grateful for" from your past experience?

_____

_____

_____

_____

_____

HOW GRATITUDE IMPROVES RELATIONSHIPS

Jennifer Wallace of the _Wall Street Journal_ spoke on _CBS This Morning_ about how gratitude can positively impact the formation of relationships.

- Gratitude helps us identify good partners.
- It helps keep us invested in these potential partners as we learn about one another.
- It helps to sustain long-term bonds, even when the relationship may be challenging.

Investing in healthy relationships includes practicing trust, which is a crucial part of healing from gaslighting. As the research suggests, gratitude is one of the more effective practices to help achieve that growth.

Telling My Story

Writing is a powerful tool that allows for cognitive, emotional, and spiritual expression. Writing itself is an act of creativity and can help us connect with feelings that may not be accessible otherwise. It can help build self-confidence and feelings of self-worth, while gaining a deeper understanding of ourselves and the world around us. The goal of gaslighting is to manipulate our sense of reality, by quieting our inner voice and the stories we tell ourselves. Writing what we feel, or know to be true, is a powerful way to reclaim these stories and connect with our truth.

EXERCISE

The following exercise provides a series of writing prompts to reflect on your experience with gaslighting. As your writing unfolds, so too will the integral parts of your story. Every detail is important and can expand your understanding of what you went through and who you are. Three different writing styles are provided: *directive writing*, *stream of consciousness*, and *future template*. Upon completing these prompts, you will have an opportunity to reflect on your emotional response to the exercise.

Using a sheet of paper, a journal, or a note-taking device, reflect and respond to each prompt in order. The prompts are designed in a specific order to enhance effective processing: you can choose to complete one prompt or all three in one sitting. Aside from prompt #2 having a one-page minimum, this exercise is not

WHAT YOU'LL LEARN
- How your experiences shaped your self-concept
- The power of storytelling to discover a greater sense of self

WHAT YOU'LL NEED
- 10 to 20 minutes when you feel relaxed and alert
- Pen and paper (or computer if typing is preferred)

about writing quality or quantity; rather, it is about the experience. For this reason, do not attempt to edit what you write.

FINAL REFLECTION

After writing your chosen prompt(s), reread them to yourself. It can help to read them out loud to further process what was written.

- What feelings do you experience when reading what you wrote?

- Did you discover anything new from what you wrote?

- Is there anything you wrote that you want to share or express to another person?

- If you chose one prompt over the other, what drew you to that prompt?

- Would you consider writing in the future and if so, how often?

_____

_____

_____

_____

To promote healing in the future, creating a practice of using one of these writing styles; *directive*, *stream of consciousness*, or *future template* writing can help with fully processing life experiences. It also helps to further protect you from gaslighting, as consistent connection with the self is crucial for standing up to abuse of many forms.

Prompt #1: Directive Writing. Tell the story of your experience with gaslighting. When did you first notice it was happening? How did it make you feel? Is there anything you would like to share with yourself in hindsight (using a non-critical and compassionate tone)?

_____

_____

_____

_____

Prompt #2: Stream of Consciousness. Write down thoughts as they come to your mind. This can pertain to your experience with gaslighting, how it feels to write your emotions, or any other thought processes that arrive organically. Try not to pause, read, or look back. If you need more space for writing, use a separate sheet of paper or write in your journal.

_____

_____

_____

_____

Prompt #3: Future Template. How does your knowledge gained from your experience with gaslighting inform what you want for your future? What kind of relationships do you believe you deserve? What red flags will you look out for going forward? What does a life without gaslighting look like?

_____

_____

_____

_____

BRINGING IT ALL TOGETHER

Learning more about yourself and understanding how valuable you are is fundamental to healing after gaslighting abuse. Dating yourself and making time to figure out what brings you a sense of joy, and then providing yourself with those things is foundational to standing up in the face of potential gaslighting abuse. You treat yourself as valuable, which you are, so that others will too.

Another aspect to building your self-worth and increasing confidence is being able to set healthy boundaries, which is made easier by feeling safe in your own body. Practicing the breath skills taught in this chapter in conjunction with carrying your body with confidence through power posing will translate your journey of healing from an idea to an action. As you notice the positive changes you are making, recognize your growth with a gratitude mindset—as opposed to focusing on how much more you still want to change. Practicing gratitude towards yourself for making these changes helps make each change, however incremental, much more attainable. As you get to know all the parts of you that were impacted by gaslighting abuse and continue to connect with your values and believe you can do hard things, you will become more equipped for self-love.

CHAPTER 9

Practice Self-Love and Embrace Who You Truly Are

This chapter explores ways to practice self-love with coping skills that strengthen your well-being and ability to thrive. Practices include yoga, breathwork, EFT tapping, IFS "parts work," EMDR, and art therapy as ways to help aid in the recovery process from gaslighting. These research-driven, therapeutic skills help rebuild your self-worth that a gaslighter intended to destroy. You will learn ways to discover more about yourself mentally, physically, and creatively, bringing you one step closer to embracing who you truly are.

Learning from Your "Parts"

WHAT YOU'LL LEARN
- A basic understanding of Dr. Richard Schwartz's Internal Family Systems Theory (IFS)
- How to learn from and appreciate what we may consider our "bad parts"

WHAT YOU'LL NEED
- 10 minutes when you feel relaxed and alert
- Pen and paper

In Dr. Richard Schwartz's Internal Family Systems (IFS) model, he explores how we are not just one unified self but rather a collection of parts making the whole. There are three types of parts: Managers (multitasker, worker, supermom, teacher, etc.), who appears high functioning until they become overworked and overwhelmed; Firefighters (emotional eater, shopaholic, angry part, procrastinator, etc.), whose role is to reduce distress as quickly as possible, even if that method is harmful; and Exiles (fears failure, worries about not feeling good enough, afraid of feeling ignored or unlovable)—these hidden parts from our past we may not even be aware of, and often have their origins in childhood trauma, interpersonal trauma, or repressed memories.

Part of self-value and confidence is learning to understand all the parts of who you are. It can help to approach all parts of you nonjudgmentally with compassion and curiosity, helping you feel safe and heard. Imagine if you shared how you felt with a friend or therapist and, instead of listening, they ignored you, walked away, or criticized your feelings. That is what happens to our parts when we reject them. They run. And without their presence, we learn nothing.

EXERCISE

In the following exercise, you will apply IFS strategies to promote healing after gaslighting and emotional abuse. Write your answers below.

1. Identify one part of you that you associate with your experience of gaslighting abuse (i.e., fearful part, defensive part, worried part, warrior part, traumatized part, survivor part). Notice any physical sensations, thoughts or emotions that arise and describe what you notice.

    _____

    _____

    _____

    _____

    _____

    _____

2. Describe the part that you associate with your experience with gaslighting in as much detail as possible. Creativity is encouraged for this exercise—there is no wrong answer.

    _____

    _____

    _____

    _____

    _____

    _____

3. With your eyes closed, take a deep breath and imagine you and this part are sitting across from each other. Ask this part where it came from (when it first came to fruition, why it arrived, and/or what its perceived "job" or role is).

_____

_____

_____

_____

_____

4. Ask the part: What do you need to feel safer? If there is resistance you can ask this part for incremental change, perhaps what it needs to feel 10 percent safer.

_____

_____

_____

_____

_____

5. Place your hand on your heart and offer love, reassurance, and support to this part. Imagine your heart expanding and pouring warmth into all the other parts too.

THINGS TO CONSIDER

· It can be difficult for some people to use visuals. If this is the case for you, simply connect with a feeling or emotion in your body.

· There may be more than one part associated with your experience. Try to choose the one who needs the most attention, or who you feel the most struggle with. You can choose to come back to this exercise in the future to support the others or repeat with the same part if there was a great deal of resistance.

· You may not feel complete resolution after this exercise, especially if the part you are working with has been deeply traumatized. In this case, use the 1 percent more method where you try to make 1 percent more change or growth. Ask yourself: What does this part need to feel 1 percent safer?

· Consider keeping a journal or running list when you discover new parts, as they are infinite.

· Notice how they differ and who and what triggers different parts to surface.

· There is much to learn with IFS so a list of supplemental readings at the end of this book offer some ways to expand on this form of self-therapy.

Confront Stress with the EMDR Spiral Technique

- How to use the EMDR Spiral Technique to confront discomfort, stress, or trauma
- The difference between dissociating from pain versus being present with it

- 15 minutes of time when you are stressed or looking to deeply relax
- A present or historic memory of feeling distress

The Spiral Technique, derived from Francine Shapiro's research-supported trauma therapy, Eye Movement Desensitization and Reprocessing (EMDR), is a wonderful tool for taking focus off disturbing thoughts or sensations that arise from stress or trauma. Unlike repressing or ignoring stress when it arises, this technique provides a safe and soothing way to cope with it in real time. It can also be used to curb anxiety or obsessive thoughts about your experience with gaslighting.

EXERCISE

The following tool can be used anytime and anywhere. It is helpful to use when you feel your Subjective Units of Distress Scale (SUDS) (see page 66) at a 4 or higher. During your first time trying this skill, find a quiet and safe space where you can be mindful as you observe how this technique impacts you.

1. Bring to mind a disturbing memory or event and notice any sensations happening in your body.

2. Close your eyes, if you feel comfortable doing so, or choose a soft gaze in front of you, if that feels safer.

3. Rate how it feels to think of the memory or experience on a scale of 0 to 10 (0 means you can remain calm, 10 means you experience intolerable distress).

4. Notice where in your body you feel tension, tightness, or unusual sensations.

5. Imagine that area of your body is moving like a spiral. Notice what direction the spiral is moving: clockwise or counterclockwise?

6. With your eyes closed, follow the spiral by moving your eyes gently around in a circle.

7. Continue for approximately 2 minutes. You can set a timer if you like or estimate by taking 10 deep breaths in and out.

8. When you feel ready to do so, use your mind to change the direction of the spiral. Notice what happens when it starts to move in the opposite direction.

9. Continue this for approximately 2 minutes.

10. Finally, re-rate your distress and journal below about what you felt when you began the spiral technique and what you noticed when you changed directions.

WAYS TO ENHANCE THE SPIRAL TECHNIQUE

- Women experience a variety of pain unique to them (pregnancy, menstruation, as well as higher rates of chronic fatigue, autoimmune disorders, and inflammation) and this skill is an excellent way to cope with that pain. Instead of using SUDS to rate emotional stress, that same scale can be used to rate physical pain.

- If you do not have 5 to 10 minutes, even a minute of this focused skill can help reduce SUDS.

- This skill can be used at the onset of a panic attack. Remain focused on slow inhales and exhales. Breath work in combination with the Spiral Technique is very powerful.

Art Therapy for Self-Love

WHAT YOU'LL LEARN

- How to use art therapy to embrace your true self
- A fun and relaxing art directive to explore what you love and who you are

WHAT YOU'LL NEED

- 20 to 30 minutes when you feel relaxed and alert
- Coloring materials (such as crayons, colored pencils, or markers)
- Paper (optional)

Art therapy, which became a clinical practice in the 1940s as an alternative method of visual communication, is a powerful tool when talking or thinking about past trauma.

According to the American Art Therapy Association, it fosters self-esteem and self-awareness, cultivates emotional resilience, promotes insight, enhances social skills, and helps to reduce and resolve conflicts and stress. Art therapy is commonly used to aid the healing process from trauma, and the following exercise focuses on improving your own self-love and self-awareness.

EXERCISE

Art therapy exercises, which are called "directives," are about the *process* and not the *product*. While making something beautiful can boost self-esteem, what is most important is what you are trying to express and how you feel when doing so. Take your time with this exercise by noticing how it feels to handle and use the art materials.

- Below you will find a blank graphic of a heart. This directive is titled "Things I love."

- Some women recovering from gaslighting report it being difficult to focus on what they love about themselves. In these cases, it can help to explore the beauty around you and remember what you love and enjoy, be those places, people, things, pets, or positive memories.

- Using a pen, fill each segment in the heart below with "loves" (if the word "love" does not resonate, you can opt for "like" or "enjoy").

- As you fill the spaces, remember *anything* that you love counts (a good movie, going for a walk, or spending time with loved ones are a few examples).

- Next, choose a variety of your favorite colors, as many or as few as you like and create a mosaic of colors, filling in each section any way that pleases you.

- When it is completed, notice the variety of colors, and take a moment to read through each "love" with gratitude.

- Finally, ask yourself these three questions to further process your piece:

  - What would I title this image?
  - What feelings does this image evoke?
  - What have I learned (or remembered) about myself?

OTHER ART THERAPY IDEAS FOR BUILDING SELF-LOVE

- Gather magazines, a piece of paper, glue, and scissors and create a collage all about yourself.

- Create an image of a safe space.

- Write an acrostic using your name. This is when you write your name down the side of a page and create a poem or composition using the first letter on each new line (e.g., Pam: **P**erseverant **A**daptable **M**usical). You can decorate the page with mindful doodles or leave it as is.

- Creating an image of a mountain, write things you have accomplished on one side and then things you wish to accomplish in the future on the other.

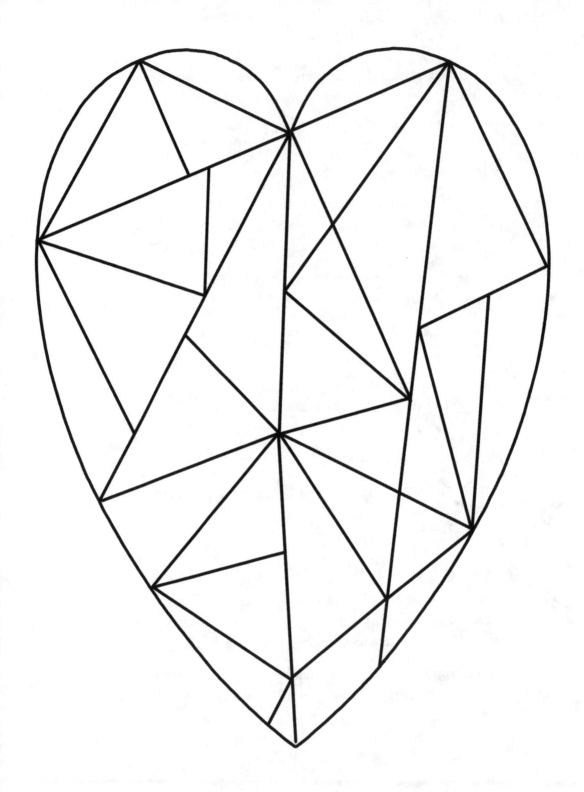

Self-Love Yoga

After the trauma of emotional abuse and gaslighting, it can feel difficult to connect with our body in a gentle way. Bessel van der Kolk, author of *The Body Keeps the Score* and pioneer of trauma research over the last 50 years, suggests the use of yoga to increase the relationship between body and self as a non-medical way to heal from trauma. Yoga truly does help to "heal the issues in our tissues" and has the potential to enhance the relationship with our breath, body, and mind, all while providing a loving practice to increase physical wellness, reduce inflammation, and help regulate stress hormones.

EXERCISE

The following are a series of yoga poses that encourage self-compassion. Take your time, spending 1 to 2 minutes per posture, if possible. This practice uses a style called *Yin*, which is a slow form of yoga based on traditional Chinese medicine.

The three tenants of Yin Yoga are:

1. Stillness: try to remain as still as possible and allow yourself to slow down in each position.

2. Breath: focus on slow inhales and exhales; with the exhale encouraging your muscles to relax more deeply.

3. Edge: this is where self-love is crucial. Do not push yourself too hard or give up on yourself too soon. Find a position you can hold in stillness but that is also comfortably challenging.

WHAT YOU'LL LEARN
- How the practice of yoga can be used to express self-love
- A gentle series of postures that encourage self-compassion and grounding

WHAT YOU'LL NEED
- 15 to 25 minutes when you feel relaxed and alert (the option to repeat the practice leads to a longer time commitment)
- Comfortable clothing you can move in
- Yoga mat (or towel)

DOWNWARD DOG

From a kneeling position, feet at hip-distance apart, biceps in line with your ears, hands firmly rooted in the ground, send your hips up towards the sky. It is not important that your legs be straight, but simply work towards that.

Self-love practice: Focus your energy on breathing into the crown (or top) of your head. When we struggle with self-doubt, our mind can become depleted of energy. This posture helps restore this. Hold this posture as close to a minute as you can.

Self-care option: If your arms become tired before the one minute is up, move to the next posture.

CHILD'S POSE

Allow your knees to separate and send your hips back between your legs until you feel an elongating of your lower back. Allow your forehead to rest on the floor and extend your neck as you stretch your arms long above your head. Inch your fingertips further up to open your thoracic spine.

Self-care option: Put a towel or extra padding under your knees, if needed.

Self-love practice: Feel your body let go into the floor and imagine any negative thoughts spilling out your forehead into the Earth. Breathe slowly and deeply into the back of your heart center.

BUTTERFLY POSE

Sitting with your feet together and your knees spread apart, extend your spine, and take a deep inhale. On your exhale, fold over your legs until you feel a comfortable stretch.

Self-care option: Place folded up towels under your knees to support your legs on either side.

Self-love practice: Take slow deep breaths while imagining you are hugging your heart, protecting it with your energy.

SPHINX POSE

Move onto your stomach and keep your toes stretched long behind you. Firm the top of your legs into the ground and press your hips downward. Press up with your hands, remain gentle with your lower back, and then rest each forearm on the ground. Extend your neck and find a soft gaze in front of you.

Self-care option: If you feel strained in the lower back, release your arms and fold your hands one on top of the other. Rest your forehead on top of your hands and breath into your lower back.

Self-love practice: Relax your jaw and imagine you are opening your heart center in this posture. Envision being open to any loving energy you or the universe has to offer.

SAVASANA

Your final posture is intended to calm your entire nervous system, calm your mind, and reduce any stress you are carrying in your body. Roll onto your back and begin by stretching your legs and arms out wide—take up as much space as you need. If you feel comfortable doing so, close your eyes. Inhale deeply and feel the back of your body connect with the ground below you. Imagine you are relaxing each part of your body, starting at the top of your head and moving down towards your toes.

Self-care option: Place a rolled-up towel or bolster under your knees to take the strain off your lower back.

Self-love practice: In this final resting pose, remind yourself that you have nowhere to be, no one to be, and nothing you have to change. You are worthy of love in this moment simply because you are you. With each inhale, bring in love, and with each exhale, release anything that does not serve you.

EFT Tapping for Pain, Stress, and Trauma

EFT tapping was first developed in the 1970s when doctors began exploring the use of acupressure stimulation to deal with stress, fear, and phobias. The technique was formally founded in the 1990s by Stanford engineer Gary Craig, and is a brief intervention that combines physical stimulation by tapping acupressure points with the tips of your fingers. Acupressure points are powerfully sensitive areas of the body that bring relief when pressure is applied. The practice helps reduce stress and negative emotions by stating the issue you want to work on (exposure), responding with affirmation (self-love), all while tapping (somatic/physical stimulation) on meridian points (the pathways in the body that help energy, otherwise known as Qi, flow and circulate when it is unblocked). After completing EFT, people report feeling more relaxed and notably less anxious with a marked reduction in racing thoughts. In a large-scale study on anxiety, it was found that, after only three sessions, research participants found more relief from tapping as compared to cognitive behavioral therapy alone. Furthermore, a study of veterans using EFT to deal with the symptoms of PTSD found the therapy reduced PTSD symptoms for 63 percent of the research participants after 10 or fewer sessions.

WHAT YOU'LL LEARN
- How to implement Emotional Freedom Technique (EFT) and why it works
- A variety of issues and situations that EFT can be useful for

WHAT YOU'LL NEED
- 5 minutes of uninterrupted time
- An issue, thought, or sensation you would like to resolve or address

EXERCISE

Below you will find the diagram for implementing EFT tapping to help deal with your own stress or emotional pain. All points are listed in sequential order. You can perform all 5 EFT steps in just 5 minutes.

1. Take a deep breath in and begin tapping with the tips of your fingers on point #1. Tapping should be firm enough to create pressure but not cause pain and the pace can be quick and repetitive. Remain on each point as long as it feels good.

2. As you continue tapping, identify an issue (perhaps a negative thought, sensation, or memory) that is causing distress. Identify a name for it (in other words, a feeling, such as loneliness, poor self-esteem, anger).

3. Rate the intensity from 1 to 10 (10 being the most distressed): _____

4. As you continue moving through the points and tapping, connect with your breath and be present with how your body is feeling. When you feel ready you can use a comforting phrase such as "Even though I feel triggered, I will allow myself to become calm and relaxed," or "Even though I feel stress, I still love and accept myself."

5. Continue moving through all points again as you repeat your chosen phrase (in your mind or out loud if desired) at least three times for each point.

6. Re-rate the intensity of your distress: _____

Tapping Points

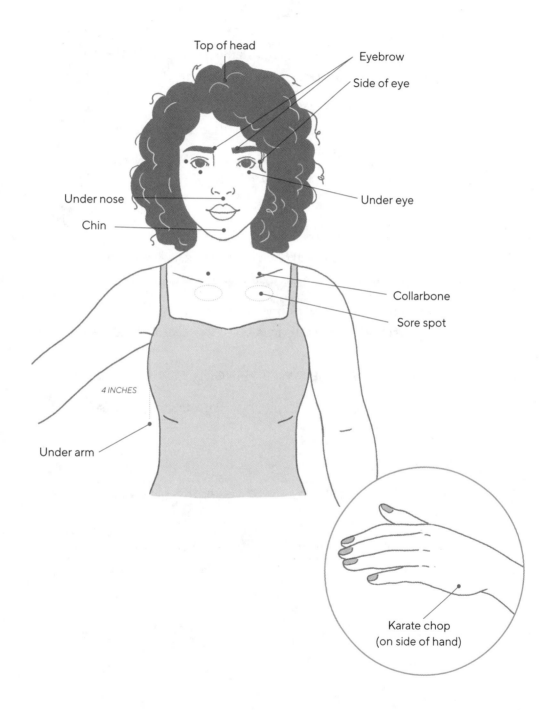

Top of head

Eyebrow

Side of eye

Under nose

Chin

Under eye

Collarbone

Sore spot

4 INCHES

Under arm

Karate chop
(on side of hand)

CONSIDERATIONS FOR TAPPING

- Returning to the tapping point at the top of the head, which coordinates with the "crown chakra," can help you create a more positive outlook on life, ground you, and make the practice feel "complete" (although you can choose to end on any point).

- You can choose to leave out points that do not feel comfortable or as therapeutic. Your body is interconnected, so tapping one acupressure point will positively impact others.

- Tapping has been researched now for nearly 30 years and has been found to bring relief for anxiety, depression, PTSD, and chronic pain, among other ailments.

- Therapists (myself included) often use tapping in sessions to help ground our clients who are struggling.

- Because tapping can be performed on yourself, it is a wonderful way to express self-love and is always an accessible form of self-care.

SAMPLE PHRASES TO USE FOR TAPPING

- "Even though I feel _____, I deeply and completely accept myself."

- "Even though I am anxious about _____, I completely accept how I feel."

- "Even though I feel out of control, I fully and completely accept myself."

- "Even though I cannot regulate my stress, I choose to relax and accept this moment."

BRINGING IT ALL TOGETHER

This chapter was created as a love letter of sorts, allowing you to not simply think about ways to show care to yourself but also put self-love into practice. Knowing what works best for you in the face of stress can further protect you from future gaslighting. Because gaslighters target insecurities, the deeper in love you are with yourself, the more you can actively guard yourself from potential abusers. Remember that forgiving yourself and having self-compassion is another form of self-love that is crucial for thriving after gaslighting. Because forgiveness can mean so many things to different people, there will be a tool to help with this complex form of self-love in the next chapter.

In the meantime, you can continue learning about yourself and loving yourself with the practices learned in this chapter. Experimenting at different times to see what works best to deal with different issues is another way to further understand who you are. Being able to turn to ourselves for care, validation, and support is a powerful way to safeguard against future potential gaslighters.

CHAPTER 10

Establish Trust and Healthy Relationships

Learning to trust again after gaslighting abuse can be difficult, whether trusting yourself or within another relationship. This process should be done incrementally and at your own pace. I explore with clients what it looks like to trust another person or yourself just 10 percent more, as opposed to diving 100 percent all in. This way, you keep your footing.

This chapter will increase your confidence and sense of safety with trusting again. The skills begin introspectively, rebuilding the foundation of self-trust. When you feel ready, the final exercises encourage you to explore future relationships you want and deserve, as well as assess any unresolved issues you wish to forgive and let go of.

Trust Your Gut–Manipura Chakra Exercise

Beginning new relationships and learning to trust again after gaslighting can feel like an uphill battle. The process can be slow, so patience is essential. If you pay close attention to how you feel after gaslighting, you can have a greater understanding of what you *do not* want in a future relationship. Being in tune with your gut instinct will better help you identify potential red flags or discomfort you feel in the earlier stages of getting to know someone. The following exercise will use Yogic chakra theory to help balance and connect you with your gut instinct, followed by an opportunity to reflect on that experience through journaling.

EXERCISE

In Yogic tradition, our gut is in the Third Chakra (Manipura), which is said to be where motivation, confidence, intentionality, and willpower are created. Western medicine has discovered that 90 percent of our body's serotonin (the "happy hormone") is created in our gut, so anything we can do to help balance our gut has the potential to positively impact our mental health as well. Deep, focused breathing can help increase the energy in our gut by increasing our metabolism; keep this in mind when performing the following meditation.

Manipura Gut Instinct Meditation

- Begin by sitting or standing tall, ideally in the sun, or a bright space, and close your eyes.

- With your arms by your sides, inhale deeply through your nose and turn your attention inward.

- Exhale through pursed lips and notice the ground beneath your feet and the space above your head.

- On your next inhale, slowly draw your arms up to the sky; visualize a bright yellow light emanating from the center of your abdomen.

- As you exhale, slowly lower your arms in one fluid motion.

- Continue this flow, feeling the yellow chakra color grow bigger with each inhale and brighter with each exhale.

- When you feel the yellow light has grown as bright and big as it can, extend your arms overhead, imagining your fingertips grazing the sky.

- Finally, allow your arms to float back to your sides and follow your natural breath.

- When you are ready, open your eyes. Sense the power you created in this practice.

Once you open your eyes, take a moment to reorient yourself to the space around you. When you are ready, answer the following questions:

What do I feel in my body when I am connected with the power of my gut instinct?

_____

_____

_____

How is this feeling different from the way I feel when I am uncertain?

_____

_____

_____

What types of people or behaviors cause my gut to lose its sense of power?

_____

_____

_____

What are specific red flags I will allow my gut to watch out for?

_____

_____

_____

The Six Stages of Internal to External Forgiveness

WHAT YOU'LL LEARN

- How forgiveness serves your journey of trusting others after gaslighting abuse
- The six stages of forgiveness and where you find yourself in the process

WHAT YOU'LL NEED

- Recollection of a person or situation you would like to forgive
- Pen and paper

The fear of being hurt again breeds mistrust of others and leads to a shielding process, particularly if the pain is still raw and tenuous. Much like the stages of grief, there are also stages of forgiveness, and each of us moves through these stages at our own pace.

It is commonly believed that forgiveness is not for the person who hurt you, but rather for yourself. This is true, but with nuances. Forgiveness begins *internally* as self-compassion, release of pain, and letting go of defense mechanisms that have both protected you and caused potential suffering. Once you experience internal forgiveness, then it is conceivable to direct forgiveness towards others.

External forgiveness happens in the last three stages and it comes in the form of "giving" or "granting" forgiveness to others. It is crucial to remember that externally forgiving does *not* mean condoning what was done to you or giving the other person permission to hurt you again; rather, it is the processing of breaking free from the tethered connection to this person (or group) and what was done to you.

The exercise below will help you explore the six stages of forgiveness. Identify which one currently you find yourself in (knowing that it is normal to move back and forth, as healing is not linear) and provide reflection questions for each stage.

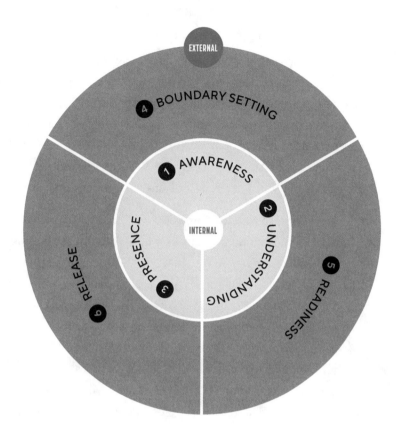

EXERCISE

Internal Forgiveness Process

1. **Awareness: Know what or who hurt you.** During this stage, the main objective is acceptance. After trauma, it can be difficult to admit the horrible thing done to you, especially if it was done by someone meant to keep you safe, but the act of acknowledging the experience is powerful. You do not have to remember all the details; anything you know, feel, or recall is your story and does not need to be confirmed by others, although you may find the desire to process with others as you move through the stages.

2. **Understanding: Know how they hurt you.** In this stage, it can help to write the experience as a story or to create an image if artistic expression feels safer. It is important to depersonalize who they are from the

way they hurt you; in other words, separate the awful actions from the person. This allows for objectivity and perspective on your behalf, thus allowing for compassion. Compassion is not condoning what they did, but rather allowing you to see *why* they did what they did. It is not an excuse but rather an explanation. As Michelle Rad explored in her *HuffPost* article on the stages of forgiveness, "Excuses remove the element of responsibility, but explanations create compassion."

3. **Presence: Be willing to feel the impact.** The third stage involves being aware of what holding the burden of unforgiveness is doing to you. Not forgiving can feel like a sickness, as anger, resentment, hate, and other negative emotions negatively impact the immune system and other aspects of energy in the body. We learn to ignore internal pain to cope, which just prolongs the healing process. If you need help being present with your anger, practices taught in this book can help, such as using the EMDR spiral technique, meditation, or checking in with your SUDS. This stage is where many people find themselves stuck because being present with pain is difficult. It is beneficial not to rush yourself and rather remain in this stage for as long as you need. Some energy healers practice the art of "cord cutting," which can be done by imagining cutting the emotional tie the other person has with you. Releasing the negative connection makes it safer to process your experience and more towards external forgiveness.

External Forgiveness Process

4. **Boundary setting: Fortify yourself.** In this stage, you take knowledge learned from the previous three stages and apply it to healthy boundary setting. This stage is especially difficult if the perpetrator is still in your life (a family member or boss at work), and the journal prompts below will explore various types of boundaries needed in order to create a sense of safety. Transitioning to external forgiveness

is only possible when you feel safe. Some boundaries may include ending a relationship, setting limits on how often you are willing to be around a person, determining what personal information you are willing to share, or setting limits on behaviors you do not condone in the future. The negative connotation around the word "ultimatum" needs to be eradicated from this stage because you have the right to make demands regarding what you don't want in a relationship and to identify consequences if someone does not respect your boundaries. For some, it is not safe to stand up to someone who hurt you, so this entire stage can be done as an internal practice. For others, you can assert yourself through written or verbal expression. Only you know the level of safety you feel with the person or group.

5. **Determine readiness to forgive.** You have arrived. You have identified who hurt you, what they did, how it is impacting you to hold anger, how you can benefit from releasing this anger, and the boundaries you need in order to feel safe. Now is the time to determine if you are ready to forgive. If the answer is "no," stay here and continue the work on the previous four stages. Some people remain in the first four stages indefinitely, but as long as they are processing in the stage they are at they are healing. If you feel ready to move towards externally forgiving (granting or declaring forgiveness) you may want to practice how you will express this.

6. **Release the burden.** At this stage, you have chosen to forgive. There are various ways to do this:

   - DEAR MAN
   - Write a letter
   - Create an art piece about the offense and, if productive, destroy it for catharsis
   - Share you desire to forgive with another safe person (without speaking to the actual perpetrator)
   - Speak to them directly (if they are a safe person)

- Role play with an empty chair (as a symbol for this person sitting with you)
- Practice Loving-Kindness Meditation for this person

Whichever way you choose to forgive, the positive benefits exist. Some find resolution or improved relationships after forgiveness, as the negative energy, pain, and unhealthy focus is released. Most importantly, you are the one who will be free; what happens to the other person is not part of the six stages—the focus is you.

The following journal prompts will assist in working through the six stages of forgiveness. Options include starting at the first stage and then progressing to where you are now, or going directly to the stage you are currently in.

Stage 1: Who and what hurt me? What was my relationship with this person before they hurt me and what has happened in that relationship since?

_____

_____

_____

_____

Stage 2: Tell the story of what they did in the third person, as if you were watching it on a movie screen. Think of this person as a character in a film; what would motivate their hurtful actions?

_____

_____

_____

_____

Stage 3: What thoughts, feelings, and/or physical sensations occur when thinking of how you were hurt? How would it feel to release this from your body? What are the potential benefits for your body, mind, and spirit if you were to do so? You can also create an image (either mentally or with art materials) of what not holding this pain would look like.

_____

_____

_____

_____

_____

Stage 4: What boundaries do I need with this person? What am I willing to share versus withhold about my life when it comes to this person? Should I end my relationship with this person? Who will help me keep these boundaries (perhaps a supportive family member, co-worker, therapist or even law enforcement)? What actions must I take to set these boundaries?

_____

_____

_____

_____

_____

Stage 5: Do I want to forgive? In what ways do I feel ready and how do I not? If I am not ready, which stage do I feel I am currently in? How can I practice self-compassion if I do not feel ready?

_____

_____

_____

_____

Stage 6: What does it mean for me to forgive? Do I want to share my thoughts with the person/group who hurt me? If I plan to speak to them, what would I like to say? If I choose to write to them, what would I say? (The next tool, "The Unsent Letter," provides an opportunity to write such a letter.) If I use DEAR MAN, what would that sound like? If I choose to meditate or mentally forgive, how could that experience help me?

_____

_____

_____

_____

Finally, remember this: forgiveness is part of the healing process and part of learning to trust others and feel safe in relationships again. Good or bad, we carry our history into the future with us. The act of forgiving does not permit others to hurt you again, but it does allow you to become more open to those who will protect your heart.

The Unsent Letter

One of the difficult parts of trusting others after gaslighting abuse is that it is not always safe to confront the person who hurt you. Many women I work with find letter writing, even if they do not intend to send the letter, to be a cathartic practice that helps aid this process. Writing your emotions can offer clarity about a situation and release negative feelings about the other person. Research by Cambridge University found that creative writing improves psychological well-being, reduces depression symptoms, improves PTSD symptoms, reduces blood pressure, and improves immune system function. The following exercise engages you in the power of writing so you too can benefit from processing your own relationship or experience.

EXERCISE

For this exercise, you can write below or expand your writing on a separate piece of paper. If it is more comfortable to type, that is fine as well.

1. Describe the situation you are going to write about and who the letter will be addressed to.

_____

_____

_____

_____

WHAT YOU'LL LEARN
- A skill for processing unresolved feelings with others
- The power of narrative therapy techniques and how to safely "metabolize" thoughts and feelings

WHAT YOU'LL NEED
- 10 to 20 minutes when you feel relaxed and alert
- A conflict or relationship you have wanted to address but have yet to
- Pen and paper

2. Next rate your current SUDS from 1 to 10 (with 10 being most stressed about the situation).

_____

_____

_____

_____

3. On a separate piece of paper, taking as much time as you need, write to the person you are struggling with. Remember, this person does not have to read this letter. Do not worry about your letter being "well written," as this is a creative exercise, and the process of writing is more important than the quality of writing.

_____

_____

_____

_____

4. Once you are done writing, take a moment to read what you wrote. You may choose to read it out loud, allowing for verbal expression of your emotions.

_____

_____

_____

_____

5. Now re-rate your SUDS from 1 to 10 after completing your letter.

_____

ENHANCING YOUR THERAPEUTIC WRITING EXERCISE

- If you think it is a safe option, you may want to share the letter with the person you wrote to.

- If you choose not to share your letter with this person, sharing it with a friend or therapist can offer further validation and catharsis.

- As mentioned before, the act of reading it out loud can feel powerful. Try reading it to an "empty chair" (a technique from Gestalt Therapy) and imagine the person it is meant for sitting there.

- You can choose to burn or destroy the letter.

- You can create artwork out of it. I had a client once cut her letter up and create a collage out of all the words in the shape of a butterfly, which for her symbolized healing.

- Your letter may motivate changes you want to make regarding this relationship. If possible, make those changes, or potentially end the relationship.

- Journal about your experience and how it made you feel.

Compassion Meditation

WHAT YOU'LL LEARN

- The power of compassion when healing from gaslighting abuse
- How to implement Metta meditation to increase well-being and move towards forgiveness at your own pace

WHAT YOU'LL NEED

- 10 minutes of your uninterrupted time
- A quiet space where you can be alone (even your car will do!)

Resentments can create a hardening of the mind and body that make it difficult to feel safe and open in future relationships. While forgiveness is not always a concept we are ready to approach, a universally beneficial step to take is practicing compassion. The following exercise is a loving-kindness meditation derived from the Yogic Metta meditation, where you first experience self-compassion and then move towards compassion for others.

EXERCISE

1. Find a comfortable position. Spend a few moments focusing on your breath and concentrating on relaxing the muscles in your body.

2. When you feel ready, start by focusing on yourself and slowly repeat the following phrases in your head: "May I be happy." "May I be healthy." "May I be safe." "May I be at ease."

3. Next, focus on someone you care for and repeat the phrases: "May you be happy." "May you be healthy." "May you be safe." "May you be at ease."

4. Now choose a neutral person—someone you see regularly but may not know well—and repeat the same wishes for that person.

5. Next, you can choose to provide well wishes for a group of people, animals, nations, and so forth.

6. Finally, choose a person who you are struggling with and provide the same wishes for them. (It can help to imagine this person as a baby or young child if conjuring an image of their present self is too difficult.)

CONSIDERATIONS FOR LOVING-KINDNESS MEDITATION

- Allow for space and time between each transition.

- You can choose to begin specifically where you feel the most need, such as the person you are struggling with.

- Simply wishing well is beneficial. Positive changes made in your mindset can help improve your current or future relationships, allowing you to enjoy being around others.

- Compassion helps build the ability to trust others.

Non-Negotiables List

WHAT YOU'LL LEARN

• How to harness the Law of Attraction to get what you want in your future relationships

• A way to identify and focus on the things you do or do not want in future relationships

WHAT YOU'LL NEED

• 10 minutes when you feel relaxed and alert

• Pen and paper

Who and what we focus our energy on and how we think and feel all have an impact on forming healthy future relationships. The impact our thoughts and feelings have on our lives is explained by the Law of Attraction which states that *what you focus your energy on is what will come back to you.* As we explored in Chapter 7 on goal setting, focusing on what you don't want (which many of us tend to do especially after experiencing trauma) does not bring you closer to what we do want.

Because gaslighting can negatively impact awareness of your inner desires, many women who are recovering from gaslighting struggle to identify what kind of partner or relationship they want in the future. The following exercise gives you time to recognize what you want in a future partner or relationship, which is an important step in feeling empowered to make these choices going forward.

EXERCISE

For this exercise, you will create your personal *non-negotiables list*. Take a moment to think of anything and everything you would like to have in a future partner (feel free to apply the list to a friendship relationship as well). Nothing is off-limits. Be as picky as possible. This is your private space to be imaginative. Women I work with identify desires that range from physical features, financial status, spiritual practice, cultural background, personality traits, and even specifics like a person who keeps their car clean!

If you struggle to identify enough items to fill the list, remind yourself of the power of "emotional individuation" we previously explored. Part of recovering from gaslighting includes remembering what you do and do not want. If you cannot fill in the list completely in one sitting, keep it available and come back to it when an idea comes to mind. Some find it helpful to ask a trusted friend or therapist to help them generate ideas, keeping in mind that the list should feel true and authentic to what is important to you.

MY NON-NEGOTIABLES LIST

1. _____

2. _____

3. _____

4. _____

5. _____

6. _____

7. _____

8. _____

9. _____

10. _____

11. _____

12. _____

13. _____

14. _____

15. _____

16. _____

17. _____

18. _____

19. _____

20. _____

NEXT STEPS WITH YOUR NON-NEGOTIABLES LIST

- You can specify "non-starters" from your list by underlining anything that would completely eliminate a potential relationship. For example, if having a similar faith is crucial for your relationship, underline it. This does not mean your preference for someone being "tall" is any less important, but it may be something you would overlook for the right person. There is *no limit* to how many things are non-starters. For some, the entire list is a requirement. This is great, as it means you are voicing your desires, which is part of recovering from gaslighting!

- Place a copy of your list somewhere you will see it often. Make it the wallpaper on your phone, put the list on your refrigerator or mirror, or put it in a keepsake box you frequently use. One of my clients placed a copy under the bed where she slept because she felt it helped her focus on it when she was dreaming.

- When starting a new relationship, revisit your list and assess if this person meets your standards.

- Revisit your list at times of growth or change; it's an organic document that can grow and change with you.

- Share your list with people you trust. Voicing your desire further helps you focus on it.

- Remember—you deserve everything you desire! Learning to trust this statement is difficult after gaslighting but it is also part of the healing process.

BRINGING IT ALL TOGETHER

The work done in this chapter was not simply about learning to let go, trust or connect with others; it was also about acknowledging and reaffirming your own values and going inward and learning more about what you want and how to set boundaries with people and situations that do not serve you. Part of trusting others means trusting yourself. Through meditation, writing, and learning about the stages of forgiveness and the practice of compassion, you can move forward after gaslighting abuse, knowing that you are fortified with a heightened sense of self-awareness and self-worth. You can always come back and revisit this chapter and these skills any time you need support or a reminder of how very important you truly are.

Conclusion

The more you focus on healing and thriving, the brighter and wider your light will shine. You become inspirational, allowing you to empower not only yourself but those around you. Gaslighters want to strip you of your self-worth and confidence, but committing to what you learned in this book is a way to say "I love myself," which is the most awesome form of rebellion. Be a rebel!

Caring for yourself, healing, and thriving after gaslighting abuse will attract the right people and propel those away who are not ready for your light. Be grateful for the ending of a bad relationship, even if it feels painful, because this is where your power lies. A healthy connection is one where you can love yourself as much as you love the other person, and at times, even more.

As Robin Arzón, inspirational instructor and speaker from Peloton, asks, "Are you willing to join the self-love club with me!?" As women, let's band together, protect each other, and call gaslighting out for what it is—a means to take away our power. Boundaries, self-love, self-respect, and unification with others who believe in you is powerful. Be powerful!

Take a deep breath. Pause and reflect on what you learned. I am forever grateful you found this book and that you took this journey with me. May you be happy, may you be healthy, may you be empowered, and may you be at peace.

Resources

Anxiously Attached: Becoming More Secure in Life and Love
by Jessica Baum
This book serves as a road map for building strong and secure relationships for those who struggle with anxiety in their romantic connections. Readers will learn practical and holistic approaches for overcoming anxious attachment issues to discover happier, more fulfilling relationships.

Better Than Before: What I Learned About Making and Breaking Habits—to Sleep More, Quit Sugar, Procrastinate Less, and Generally Build a Happier Life by Gretchen Rubin
This is *the* book for helping you get unstuck in a way that makes so much sense for women. Rubin's compassionate tone and wealth of knowledge help you understand how to make changes based on your specific tendency, instead of trying to conform to how things work for others.

The Body Keeps the Score: Brain, Mind, and Body in the Healing of Trauma
by Bessel van der Kolk
This comprehensive book explores the consequences of trauma, offering hope and clarity to everyone touched by its impact. Readers learn about advances in brain science, attachment research, and body awareness that inform treatments that can free trauma survivors from their struggles of their past.

Complex PTSD: From Surviving to Thriving by Pete Walker
This book serves as a tool for understanding the various trauma responses that result from complex relationship trauma. It offers specific ways to deal with these responses (*fight, flight, freeze, fawn*) when they occur.

The Gaslight Effect: How to Spot and Survive the Hidden Manipulation Others Use to Control Your Life by Dr. Robin Stern
This book has been part of the movement popularizing the term *gaslighting* and is based on Stern's experiences of treating patients within her practice.

Gaslighting: Recognize Manipulative and Emotionally Abusive People—and Break Free by Stephanie Moulton Sarkis

The author in this book is an expert on gaslighting who offers an extensive guide on a variety of gaslighters and the harm they cause. This author cares a great deal about empowering women and speaks often on the topic.

The Highly Sensitive Person's Guide to Dealing with Toxic People: How to Reclaim Your Power from Narcissists and Other Manipulators by Shahida Arabi

This book offers evidence-based skills grounded in cognitive behavioral therapy (CBT) and dialectical behavior therapy (DBT) to help you recognize and shut down common manipulation tactics used by toxic people, such as gaslighting, stonewalling, projection, covert put-downs, and love bombing. Arabi, an esteemed researcher on narcissism, helps you reclaim your power from narcissists, manipulators, and other toxic people.

Self-Compassion: The Proven Power of Being Kind to Yourself by Kristin Neff

This book answers the complex question, "How do I improve my self-esteem?" Written from an authentic and honest voice, paired with research-supported exercises, it is a crucial book for your self-worth toolbox.

Speak: Find Your Voice, Trust Your Gut, and Get from Where You Are to Where You Want to Be by Tunde Oyeneyin

This book is a beautiful exploration of what it means to believe in yourself despite your past experiences and what it means to listen to your inner voice when choosing your future challenges.

What I Wish I Knew: Surviving and Thriving After an Abusive Relationship by Amelia Kelley, PhD, and Kendall Ann Combs

This book offers an intimate and honest account of a survivor (Combs) during and after her abusive relationship. Her story is supported by a therapist (Dr. Kelley) with insights, skills, and knowledge about how to recognize abuse before it is too late.

The Divorce Survival Guide Podcast

In this *New York Times* recommended podcast, certified coach Kate Anthony offers a decade's worth of experience helping women (with children in particular) make the most difficult decision of their lives: *Should I stay or should I go?*

The Mel Robbins Podcast

If you are looking for a podcast to help promote positive change and self-empowerment, this is the one to listen to. With humor, honesty, and authenticity, Mel Robbins speaks about the topics we all only think about.

National Domestic Violence Hotline

For immediate help or assistance, call 800-799-SAFE (7233), text START to 88788, or visit the website thehotline.org. Open 24/7 with 200-plus languages through interpretation services.

References

PART 1

Arabi, S. *"5 Sneaky Things Narcissists Do to Take Advantage of You"* (2014). thoughtcatalog.com/shahida-arabi/2014/08/5-sneaky-things-narcissists-do-to-take-advantage-of-you.

Arabi, S. "Gaslighting: Disturbing Signs an Abuser Is Twisting Your Reality" (2017). thoughtcatalog.com/shahida-arabi/2017/11/50-shades-of-gaslighting-the-disturbing-signs-an-abuser-is-twisting-your-reality.

Arabi, S. "Narcissistic and psychopathic traits in romantic partners predict post-traumatic stress disorder symptomology: Evidence for unique impact in a large sample." *Personality and Individual Differences*, 201 (2023). doi.org/10.1016/j.paid.2022.111942.

Ashton, Jennifer. "Data Shows Women, People of Color Affected Most by 'Medical Gaslighting.'" ABC News, April 6, 2022. abcnews.go.com/GMA/Wellness/video/data-shows-women-people-color-affected-medical-gaslighting-83905811.

Covey, Stephen R. *The Seven Habits of Highly Effective People*. New York: Free Press, 1989.

Cukor, George, dir. *Gaslight*. 1944; Beverly Hills, CA: Metro-Goldwyn-Mayer Studios.

Doychak, Kendra, and Chitra Raghavan. "'No Voice or Vote:' Trauma-Coerced Attachment in Victims of Sex Trafficking." *Journal of Human Trafficking* 6, no. 3 (2020): 339–57. doi: 10.1080/23322705.2018.1518625.

Hamilton, Patrick. *Gas Light: A Victorian Thriller in Three Acts*. London: Constable and Company Ltd., 1938.

Kaylor, Leah. "Psychological Impact of Human Trafficking and Sex Slavery Worldwide: Empowerment and Intervention." American Psychological Association. September 2015. apa.org/international/pi/2015/09/leah-kaylor.pdf.

Moyer, Melinda Wenner. "Women Are Calling Out Medical Gaslighting." *New York Times*, March 31, 2022.

National Domestic Violence Hotline. thehotline.org.

Ni, Preston. "7 Stages of Gaslighting in a Relationship." *Psychology Today*, April 30, 2017. psychologytoday.com/us/blog/communication-success/201704/7-stages-gaslighting-in-relationship.

Oxford English Dictionary Online. s.v. "art, n. 1." oed.com.

"Recognizing, Addressing Unintended Gender Bias in Patient Care." Duke Health. physicians.dukehealth.org/articles/recognizing-addressing-unintended-gender-bias-patient-care.

"Refusing to Provide Health Services." Guttmacher Institute. December 1, 2022. guttmacher.org/state-policy/explore/refusing-provide-health-services.

Ruíz, E. "Cultural Gaslighting." *Hypatia* 35, no. 4 (2020): 687–713.

Tawwab, Nedra. *Set Boundaries, Find Peace: A Guide to Reclaiming Yourself.* New York: TarcherPerigee, 2021.

Thompson, Dennis. "'Medical Gaslighting' Is Common, Especially Among Women." UPI Health News, July 15, 2022. upi.com/Health_News/2022/07/15/medical-gaslighting/1951657890917.

PART 2

American Society for the Positive Care of Children. americanspcc.org.

Baum, Jessica. *Anxiously Attached: Becoming More Secure in Life and Love.* New York: Penguin, 2022.

Bowlby, J. "Attachment Theory and Its Therapeutic Implications." *Adolescent Psychiatry* 6 (1978): 5–33.

Clear, James. *Atomic Habits: Tiny Changes, Remarkable Results: An Easy & Proven Way to Build Good Habits & Break Bad Ones.* New York: Avery, 2018.

Clear, James. "Habit Score Card." Accessed November 13, 2022. jamesclear.com/habits-scorecard.

Finkelhor, D., A. Shattuck, H. Turner, and S. Hamby. "The Adverse Childhood Experiences (ACE) Study." *American Journal of Preventative Medicine* 14 (2015): 245–58.

Flaherty, S. C., and L. S. Sadler. "A Review of Attachment Theory in the Context of Adolescent Parenting." *Journal of Pediatric Health Care* 25, no. 2 (March–April 2011): 114–21.

"Keeping Your Eyes on the Prize Can Help with Exercise, Psychology Study Finds." NYU. October 1, 2015. Accessed November 10, 2022. nyu.edu/about/news-publications/news/2014/october/keeping-your-eyes-on-the-prize-can-help-with-exercise.html.

Levine, Amir, and Rachel S. F. Heller. *Attached: The New Science of Adult Attachment and How It Can Help You Find—and Keep—Love.* New York: TarcherPerigee, 2010.

Linehan, M. M. *DBT Training Manual.* New York: Guilford Press, 2014.

McGlynn, F. D. "Systematic Desensitization." In *The Corsini Encyclopedia of Psychology*, 4th edition, edited by I. B. Weiner and W. E. Craighead (Hoboken, NJ: Wiley, 2010).

Meerwijk, Esther L., Judith M. Ford, and Sandra J. Weiss. "Brain Regions Associated with Psychological Pain: Implications for a Neural Network and Its Relationship to Physical Pain." *Brain Imaging and Behavior* 7, no. 1 (2013): 1–14.

Neff, Kristin. *Self-Compassion: The Proven Power of Being Kind to Yourself.* New York: HarperCollins, 2011.

"Patterns and Characteristics of Codependence." Co-Dependents Anonymous. 2011. coda.org/meeting-materials/patterns-and-characteristics-2011.

Raye, Ethan. "Resmaa Menakem Talks Healing Racial Trauma." *Heights*, March 28, 2021. bcheights.com/2021/03/28/resmaa-menakem-talks-healing-racial-trauma.

Rubin, Gretchen. "Four Tendencies Quiz." gretchenrubin.com/quiz/the-four-tendencies-quiz.

Tierney, John. "Do You Suffer from Decision Fatigue?" *New York Times*, August 21, 2011.

Walker, Pete. *Complex PTSD: From Surviving to Thriving: A Guide and Map for Recovering from Childhood Trauma*, 1st edition. Lafayette, CA: Azure Coyote, 2013.

Wansink, B., and J. Sobal. "Mindless Eating: The 200 Daily Food Decisions We Overlook." *Environment and Behavior* 39, no. 1 (2007): 106–23.

PART 3

"About Art Therapy." American Art Therapy Association. 2022. arttherapy.org/about-art-therapy.

Ahmed, A., R. Gayatri Devi, and A. Jothi Priya. "Effect of Box Breathing Technique on Lung Function Test." *Journal of Pharmaceutical Research International* 33, no. 58A (2021): 25–31. doi: 10.9734/jpri/2021/v33i58A34085.

Baikie, K. A., and K. Wilhelm. "Emotional and Physical Health Benefits of Expressive Writing." *Advances in Psychiatric Treatment* 11, no. 5 (2005): 338–46.

Bolton, G., S. Howlett, C. Lago, and J. K. Wright. *Writing Cures: An Introductory Handbook of Writing in Counseling and Therapy*. Hove, England: Brunner-Routledge, 2004.

Brown, Brené. *Daring Greatly: How the Courage to Be Vulnerable Transforms the Way We Live, Love, Parent and Lead*. London: Portfolio Penguin, 2013.

Chapman, Gary D. *The Five Love Languages*. Farmington Hills, MI: Walker Large Print, 2010.

Church, D., S. Stern, E. Boath, A. Stewart, D. Feinstein, and M. Clond. "Emotional Freedom Techniques to Treat Posttraumatic Stress Disorder in Veterans: Review of the Evidence, Survey of Practitioners, and Proposed Clinical Guidelines." *Permanente Journal* 21, no. 4 (2017): 16–100. doi: 10.7812/TPP/16-100.

Clinton, Hillary. *What Happened*. New York: Simon & Schuster, 2017.

Craig, G., and A. Fowlie. *Emotional Freedom Techniques*. Sea Ranch, CA: self-published, 1995.

Cuddy, Amy. "Your Body Language May Shape Who You Are." TED video, 20:46. 2014. ted.com/talks/amy_cuddy_your_body_language_may_shape_who_you_are.

Feinstein, D. "Energy Psychology: A Review of the Preliminary Evidence." *Psychotherapy: Theory, Research, Practice, Training* 45, no. 2 (2008): 199–213. doi. org/10.1037/0033-3204.45.2.199.

Macy, R. J., E. Jones, L. M. Graham, and L. Roach. "Yoga for Trauma and Related Mental Health Problems: A Meta-Review with Clinical and Service Recommendations." *Trauma, Violence, & Abuse* 19, no. 1 (2018): 35–57.

Rad, Michelle Roya. "The Five Psychological Stages of Forgiveness." HuffPost, September 11, 2011. huffpost.com/entry/psychological-stages-of-f_b_955731.

Schwartz, Richard C. *Introduction to the Internal Family Systems Model*. Oak Park, IL: Trailheads Publications, 2001.

Shapiro, Francine. *Getting Past Your Past: Take Control of Your Life with Self-Help Techniques from EMDR Therapy*. Emmaus, PA: Rodale Books, 2012.

Van der Kolk, Bessel A. *The Body Keeps the Score: Brain, Mind, and Body in the Healing of Trauma*. New York: Viking, 2014.

Wallace, Jennifer. "How Gratitude Can Improve Your Health, Happiness, and Relationships." CBS News, November 22, 2018. cbsnews.com/video/how-gratitude-can-improve-your-health-happiness-and-relationships.

Index

Page numbers in *italics* indicate illustrations.

Acknowledgments

This book would not exist without the women who inspire me—honest risk-takers who are writing, speaking, and sharing their truth with the world. Beyond the books and authors who inspire me, my writing is directly inspired by the women I have worked with in therapy throughout my years of practice. Their willingness to trust me and our relationship during the process of healing through therapy has enlightened me to the human condition and our ability to heal. You are the true warriors behind this book.

I would like to acknowledge my fierce tribe of female friends who have shaped me, inspired me, supported me, laughed with me, and always reminded me who I am. I am forever learning how to be a better version of myself because of you.

I would also like to thank my supportive husband, who took care of our children as I sat locked away in my office, writing for hours. He is a true example of a man who lifts women up and sees how impressive, inspirational, and courageous we truly are. You are what all women deserve.

Finally, I would like to thank my editors and the team at Zeitgeist and Penguin Random House for trusting me with such an important project. At a time when gaslighting has become a primary focus in our society, the literature produced must do the movement justice, and with your help I believe we have provided just that.

About the Author

Amelia Kelley, PhD, is an integrative, trauma-informed therapist with 20 years of experience as an art therapist and certified meditation and yoga instructor. She is trained in EMDR, hypnotherapy, somatic therapies, Internal Family Systems (IFS), and Brainspotting. She is a trainer, podcaster, and writer in the "science-help" field, focusing on motivation, women's issues, empowering survivors of abuse and relationship trauma, Highly Sensitive Persons, healthy living, and adult ADHD.

Dr. Kelley is an adjunct professor of counseling at Yorkville University and a nationally recognized relationship expert featured on the SiriusXM Doctor Radio program *The Psychiatry Show*, exploring the impact of gaslighting on our society. She is a coach and trainer for the SAS Work/Life Program and resident trainer for the Art Therapy Institute of North Carolina. Her private practice is part of the Traumatic Stress Research Consortium at the Kinsey Institute. She is a co-author of *What I Wish I Knew: Surviving and Thriving After an Abusive Relationship* and a regular contributing writer for the world's largest blog for HSPs, *The Highly Sensitive Refuge*. Her work has been featured in *Teen Vogue*, Scary Mommy, Yahoo! News, Well+Good, and Insider.

Follow her on Instagram @drameliakelley or visit ameliakelley.com.